MENLO PARK
HISTORICAL
ASSOCIATION

MENLO PARK
CALIFORNIA
BEYOND *the* GATE

MICHAEL SVANEVIK AND SHIRLEY BURGETT

CUSTOM & LIMITED EDITIONS
San Francisco • New York

Published 2000 by CUSTOM & LIMITED EDITIONS, San Francisco, California

Designed by Morris Jackson

Library of Congress Cataloging-in-Publication Data

Svanevik, Michael, 1942-
    Menlo Park, California : Beyond the Gate / Michael Svanevik and Shirley Burgett.
      p. cm.
    Includes index.
    ISBN 1-881529-64-9
    1. Menlo Park (Calif.)--History--Pictorial works. 2. Menlo Park (Calif.)--History.
I. Burgett, Shirley. II. Title.

F869.M54 S86 2000
979.4'69--dc21

                                                                                    00-031823

First Printing
Printed in the United States of America

PREFACE

What follows is a broad overview of Menlo Park, California. The town is primarily a residential community on the San Francisco Peninsula in San Mateo County, approximately 30 miles south of the Golden Gate.

This is a local history told in words and pictures. It is aimed at people who have never visited Menlo Park and longtime town residents as well. Our method has been to explore several aspects of general interest, noting some recurrent themes.

Countless people have contributed to the success of this historical project, far too many to thank specifically. Nevertheless, the authors feel it imperative to give individual credit to local archivists Jeanne Bone and Frank Helfrich of the Menlo Park Historical Association. Not only did they generously share treasured documents and photographs, but their unselfish donation of time, energy and, most of all, experience helped to ensure a satisfactory result.

Neither author is a Menlo Park resident. Thus the town's story is told from the standpoint of outsiders looking in.

Michael Svanevik and Shirley Burgett

The U.S. Geological Survey moved to Menlo Park in 1954.

INTRODUCTION

Any weekday at noon, traffic in the town is fierce.

Parking lots are crowded. Restaurant tables and lunch counters are full. Stylishly dressed women scurry along busy sidewalks. Professionals with briefcases and students with book bags share street corners waiting for green lights.

Menlo Park, California. Literally almost in the shadow of the Hoover Tower at Stanford University and on the doorstep of Silicon Valley.

Once upon a time a tranquil bedroom community, the town had been frequently referred to as the "Sleepy Hollow of California," but in the years after World War II, its community surged to new life.

In just over four decades, a soaring population tripled, reaching an amazing 30,400 by 1990. Writers scrambling for words to describe the Menlo Park phenomenon invariably today choose adjectives like *dynamic, affluent* and *upscale*.

A major factor contributing to this extraordinary growth has been the ever increasing prestige of Stanford University, one of the world's premier academic institutions, located just minutes from Menlo Park on the south bank of San Francisquito Creek. Since opening in 1891, the university has served as a magnet attracting creative and innovative minds as well as important institutions to the Peninsula.

One, Stanford Research Institute (SRI International since the 1970s) opened at Menlo Park in 1947. Within a few years, this remarkable facility, where engineers have developed a long list of new products ranging from kitchen detergents to the computer mouse to stealth aviation technology, by 1999 was utilizing 1.3 million square feet of work space and employing 2,000 people.

Another such institution, the U.S. Geological Survey, committed to earthquake study, map making and undersea exploration, opened its western headquarters at Menlo in 1954. Since then, as many as 1,700 have been employed there simultaneously.

Raychem Corporation, an international electronics and telecommunications firm headquartered at 300 Constitution Drive in Menlo Park had its origin there in 1957. By 1999, this vibrant company was employing 9,000, half of whom worked

This gateway came to symbolize the town of Menlo Park.

in the United States, and doing an annual business valued at $1.8 billion.

Menlo Park has played a dominating role in the futuristic world of twenty-first century super-electronic technology. Much of the money that makes Silicon Valley function is generated along Sand Hill Road in Menlo Park, where more than 40 firms control an estimated one-third of the nation's $12 billion in venture capital.

Given the town's fortuitous location, property values have skyrocketed. Modest homes that sometimes sold for $15,000 during the 1950s, were being snapped up 40 years later, often within hours of being placed on the market, for more than a million dollars.

But the factor that has contributed most to making this community a particularly popular place to live and work is that, despite its hustle and bustle and despite its genuine importance, Menlo Park still at least *seems* like a small town. The downtown, while increasingly sophisticated, in fact has changed little in 50 years. Menlo Park Hardware, a fixture on Santa Cruz Avenue since 1924, continues to be run by the same family that established it.

The name Menlo Park was applied to the area as early as 1854 when two Irish immigrants, Dennis J. Oliver and Daniel C. McGlynn built farms on the southern reaches of what had been a Mexican land grant, *Rancho de las Pulgas*. The pair hailed from Menlough, County Galway in Ireland. To mark their property, the men erected a massive arched gateway, hanging a sign on it reading "Menlo Park."

When the tracks of the Peninsula railroad reached San Francisquito Creek in 1863, for a time the end of the line, builders erected a depot across the road from the landmark sign. Quite naturally, this became known as Menlo Park Station. And long after Oliver and McGlynn were gone, the name remained.

The gateway, which predated the town itself, became an important symbol of Menlo Park. Though this unique structure was ultimately destroyed by a reckless driver in 1922, its unusual architectural design remained imprinted in the minds of pioneer residents. In 1971, when the Menlo Park Historical Association was established, the Oliver-McGlynn gate was chosen as the organization's logo.

For a number of years, the name Menlo Park applied to virtually all of San Mateo County south of Redwood City. When the town was briefly incorporated in 1874, within its boundaries were all of Menlo Park, Atherton, Ravenswood and East Palo Alto.

Milton Latham's elegant stables were the envy of the aristocratic community.

Not many decades before, Menlo Park had been a summertime sanctuary almost exclusively for the well-to-do of San Francisco. Except for notable early arrivals Isaiah C. Woods and Faxon D. Atherton, who erected elegant homes in the area during the 1850s and early 1860s, a storied epoch of the great landed estates dated from the completion of the Peninsula railroad between San Francisco and San Jose in 1864. That era continued until the turn of the twentieth century.

Sprawling houses, each with its own name, were erected by San Francisco's most powerful and influential pioneer families. The builders were the city's merchants, bankers, financiers, lumber tycoons, attorneys and mining kings. With a few exceptions, their marvelous estates were built in the exclusive Fair Oaks neighborhood of Menlo Park, a portion that later broke away to incorporate as the town of Atherton.

These were great houses run by teams of efficient servants. Numerous dissertations on the mansions are replete with minute descriptions of spacious, high-ceilinged rooms crammed with lavish European antique furnishings, exquisite wood paneling, polished parqueted floors, plush carpeting, imposing stairways, stained-glass transoms, silver bathroom fixtures, gleaming marble entryways, and fireplaces.

For the uninitiated, a first visit to the Fair Oaks section of Menlo Park was a never-to-be-forgotten experience. Landscaping was breathtaking. Estates were acclaimed for their unrivaled beauty. Behind regal entry gates were imported trees and what seemed like miles of carefully manicured lawns punctuated by ancient live oaks, brilliantly blooming flower gardens, chaste statuary and splashing fountains. The well-traveled agreed that these were some of the most outstanding gardens in America. Some featured tranquil artificial lakes with flocks of ducks or graceful long-necked swans. A few lakes were kept continually stocked with game fish for the pleasure of honored guests.

Fashionably dressed riders on thoroughbred horses cantered along miles of carefully tended bridle paths winding lazily through the wooded estates. Gaslit stables, often surmounted by elaborate clock towers, were built with rare imported woods and highlighted by silver fixtures and marble ornamentation. Impeccably kept, they often seemed as ornate as the great houses themselves.

Newspaper readers learned in 1880 that silver tycoon James C. Flood, a

James C. Flood's Linden Towers, *the largest house west of the Mississippi, was known for its palatial gardens.*

recent arrival to Menlo Park, had dispatched scores of Chinese workers to the beaches of Monterey to gather sacks of smooth white pebbles with which to pave the promenades at *Linden Towers*, his estate on Middlefield Road.

In the truest English manorial tradition, Menlo estates were self-sustaining units. An adequate number of cows provided families with milk and other dairy products. Parts of the properties were set aside for chickens. There were fruit orchards and vegetable gardens. A few had vineyards. Though families traditionally returned to San Francisco in the early fall, staffs were maintained the year round. At least once each week, estate superintendents rode the trains to the city carrying baskets of fresh vegetables, fruits, butter and eggs for a family's table.

At Menlo Park, fashionable inhabitants led decorous and salubrious lives, an existence that Stanford University President Ray Lyman Wilbur later referred to as "Eden-like." Life was unruffled by the breath of excitement. Day-to-day tranquility was broken only by afternoon teas and occasional horticultural exhibitions, when residents congregated to show one another their prized flowers.

Meanwhile, along the dusty County Road — later El Camino Real — near the railroad station, a small service community slowly developed. In 1863, the Menlo Park Villa Association, comprised of wealthy real estate entrepreneurs, offered acreage on both sides of the track for sale. This development became the town of Menlo Park.

San Francisco newspapers advertised that there were few such places within 100 miles of that bay metropolis that combined rich soil, excellent climate, and so many other natural advantages.

There was soon a hotel, a couple of boarding houses, a blacksmith and four saloons. Work on a Catholic church was not commenced in Menlo Park until 1872 and no Protestant church was built until a year later.

From the beginning, Menlo Park, both town and country, was an Irish domain. There was no larger Irish enclave anywhere on the Peninsula. Not only were the estates owned by wealthy Irishmen, but more humble men of Ireland who emigrated during the potato famine of the late 1840s and 1850s became the storekeepers and townsmen. They soon dominated, the local economy. Menlo's first genuine merchandise emporium, Duff & Doyle's general store, run by two Irishmen, opened in 1874 when the town's population was still fewer than 300.

Duff & Doyle's became the town's original merchandise emporium.

Almost immediately Duff & Doyle's became a community institution. The store stocked everything from blasting powder to silk ribbon and pickled herring. Upstairs were a dance floor, lodge room and assembly hall. Menlo's first fraternal lodge, dating from the early 1870s, was the Ancient Order of Hibernians.

Numerous Chinese, many coaxed by Southern Pacific Railroad executive Leland Stanford and Menlo Park resident Timothy Hopkins (adopted son of Mary Frances Sherwood Hopkins, widow of the transcontinental railroad builder), also found their way to the Peninsula. They worked as laborers who served the outlying estates. At the very least, most landowners employed Chinese cooks and laundrymen. By the 1880s, in town, there were a Chinese laundry, a gambling house and a number of usually-shuttered habitations. Until after the turn of the twentieth century, Chinese men with characteristic long braided queues wore traditional Asian dress; there were comparatively few Chinese women in the area. Menlo Park's Chinatown was the largest such community south of San Francisco.

Millionaire San Francisco attorney and scholar John T. Doyle, a connoisseur of fine wines, during the 1880s, established a vineyard in Cupertino and another at *Ringwood*, his Menlo estate along Middlefield Road. Italian vintner Giovanni Beltramo, patriarch of one of the town's most prominent twentieth-century families, was employed to cultivate Doyle's grapes.

Before long, Menlo Park became a mecca for scores of dirt poor Italians, predominantly single men from the Piedmont region of northern Italy. Trained as farmers and as horticulturists, they were primarily employed maintaining estate gardens, most of which became notably Italian in appearance. Though most of the gardeners lived on the land where they worked, on weekends they gravitated into town for entertainment.

Thus, from the very beginning, two radically different civilizations began to emerge in Menlo. There was Menlo Park *the country*, dominated by wealthy landowners and visited regularly by American presidents and other powerful potentates. And there was Menlo Park *the town*, comprised of lower class Irishmen, humble Italians, mysterious opium-smoking "Chinese Celestials" and a smattering of Germans and other nationalities. The well-to-do scorned the town, where the dusty streets "crawled with little urchins." They refused to identify with it, seldom visited and rarely shopped there. Most referred to the town simply as "that sordid

Country Squire Timothy Hopkins made Menlo Park floriculture into a booming business.

little village."

Through the decades, this schism between town and country continued to broaden. The wealthy commonly identified themselves as residents of Fair Oaks, not Menlo Park, and a second railroad stop was established. But powerful Southern Pacific Railroad opposed the continued use of the name Fair Oaks because there already was such a community in Sacramento County. Thus in 1912, residents of the historic and aristocratic district of Menlo Park voted to refer to their district as Atherton.

Atherton, the town, however, the borders of which twisted and dodged through Menlo Park to insure the inclusion of almost all the grand estates, was not incorporated until 1923.

The first of several pivotal historic events that began to awaken sleepy Menlo Park occurred in 1891. It wasn't that President Benjamin Harrison visited the town in April. Nor was it that young ladies were discarding traditional riding costumes in favor of knickerbockers or that mumbletypeg and rope jumping were all that seemed to be occupying juvenile minds.

Just across San Francisquito Creek on the vast properties of Leland Stanford, workers were busily applying final touches to Leland Stanford Junior Memorial University, scheduled to welcome its first class in October 1891. Since a cornerstone was laid in 1887, the university had risen on what had been Stanford's state-of-the-art horse breeding farm. Throughout 1891, virtually every newspaper published in nearby Redwood City was crammed with details and progress reports.

The town of Palo Alto had not yet been established, so, in the beginning, Menlo Park's was the nearest railroad station to the university, and the town acquired new status. Business boomed. At Duff & Doyle's, four clerks had to be hired to handle the influx of customers. New homes were under construction and vacant cottages were refurbished for the expected influx of students and professors.

Floriculture brought the town even greater acclaim. At *Sherwood Hall*, the sprawling estate of country squire Timothy Hopkins, Irish gardening wizard Michael Lynch and 43 assistants rejuvenated fruit orchards and cultivated 250 varieties of chrysanthemums in the open air. Their color and quality caused San Francisco florists to express astonishment. One chrysanthemum plant produced a bloom 20 inches in diameter.

Menlo Park kindergartners in 1893 posed on the front steps of their schoolhouse.

Fragrant odors emitting from *Sherwood Hall's* violet beds, especially on damp evenings, were immense. Five different varieties, six full acres of violets grew within sight of the great house's front door. This was the largest violet field in the nation. (The "fragrant, purple violet" was made the official flower of Menlo Park in 1982.)

As if responding to the town's newfound importance, Menlo Park Hotel proprietor Martin Kuck retained workers to undertake a complete renovation, ensuring that the hotel, a local landmark since the 1860s, remained an attractive place of rustication for summer visitors.

The Menlo Park Improvement Club called for sidewalks to end the scourge of winter mud. Water pipes were laid throughout the town. Charles Harbo, a renowned carriage painter, opened a store near the post office. In September 1891, Matthew Crowe achieved local fame. In his cornfield on the outskirts of town, one stalk reached the unheard of height of 12 feet. The next month a bicycle store opened adjacent to the barbershop. Its proprietor did brisk business renting bicycles to new arrivals in town.

During the last week of September 1891, Menlo Park was crowded with 559 expectant university students, who gathered from all over the nation. Their towering piles of trunks were stacked up on the depot platform. More students and professors came with every train.

On October 1, Leland Stanford arrived by special train, personally accompanying 2,000 distinguished guests. Ultimately a full 5,000 participants, most on foot, trudged from Menlo Park across the creek for the dedication of the new university.

Almost immediately the presence of this soon to be esteemed academic institution began to alter the course of Menlo Park history. California educators awakened to the advantages of Menlo Park. This tranquil and bucolic sanctuary was near a prominent university and the cultural advantages of a major city, but far enough from San Francisco to insure students could not be tainted by urban evil.

Three notable private academic institutions opened at Menlo in 1898. One, a school for boys, was started by noted California educator Dr. Ira D. Hoitt, A.B., M.A. Claiming that his goal was "to stimulate...manly impulses," while preparing boys for admission to "the best colleges, universities or technical schools in the

Classes at Convent of the Sacred Heart began in 1898.

land," Hoitt moved his already much acclaimed school from an earlier campus in Burlingame, reopening in the renovated *Valparaiso Park*, former estate house of the late Faxon D. Atherton.

But the school's Menlo existence was short-lived. After just a few months, the historic and now almost legendary mansion was consumed by fire. In his search for a new campus, Hoitt left the county.

Meanwhile, in August 1898, a strict order of French-speaking Roman Catholic nuns, the Mesdames of the Sacred Heart, convened classes for 23 young ladies in the then just completed Convent of the Sacred Heart, located in the grassy oak-punctuated fields west of Menlo Park. There, isolated behind red brick walls, daughters of the Peninsula's most elite Catholic families lived and studied in a well regulated, strict environment. The convent soon was recognized as the area's premier lyceum for young ladies of culture and refinement.

Simultaneously, east of Middlefield Road in the Ravenswood section of Menlo Park, workers scurried about adding final flourishes to St. Patrick's Seminary, a massive brick structure destined to become the Catholic church's most revered academic institution in the West. Under the control of French Sulpician priests, the seminary was committed to the training of Roman Catholic clergy for the western United States. Supervised by the San Francisco Archdiocese, St. Patrick's Seminary was dedicated September 20, 1898.

But the most powerful and disruptive influence on the region was the proximity of Stanford University and its ever-growing student body. At the insistence of Leland and Jane Stanford, both temperate in their views, the sale of alcoholic beverages in Palo Alto, a town established for the university in 1894, was strictly forbidden. Saloons at Mayfield, an easy walk from the campus south of San Francisquito Creek, were padlocked.

But at Menlo Park, where the burgeoning Irish and Italian populations viewed drinking almost as an inalienable right, saloons not only continued to operate, they proliferated. Before the ultimate ban on these drinking emporiums in 1910, Menlo Park boasted 18. Athletes, fraternity boys and students in general faithfully invaded Menlo's drinking spas on weekends. Public drunkenness resulting in rowdy and often lewd behavior became common. Town residents regarded Stanford men as vicious drinkers and a curse on the quietude of their village. Catholic leaders

Saloons served as magnets attracting university students.

complained that innocent young ladies from the convent and cassock-clad seminarians from St. Patrick's were being harassed and embarrassed.

A second pivotal event in the history of the town came with the outbreak of World War I. For all citizens, America's entry into the war in the spring of 1917 was unsettling. But for the people of tranquil Menlo Park what happened there came as a traumatic shock from which the old town never fully recovered. When war was declared, the population was still under 2,000. But noting Menlo Park's almost ideal climate, which would assure year-round military training, the U.S. War Department designated the town as the center of Camp Fremont, one of the nation's 14 new Army basic training facilities.

By the end of summer 1917, an enormous tent city had come into being and every arriving train disgorged new recruits. The military headquarters were near the intersection of what became El Camino Real and Roble Avenue.

Proprietors of large San Francisco stores clamored for space to create Menlo Park branches. Restaurants and ice cream shops proliferated. A movie house sprang up overnight. The town bulged with a temporary population of almost 43,000.

Day and night the rattle of machine gun fire and the blasts of artillery echoed from the hills west of town. Soldiers awakened and bunked to the penetrating sounds of bugles. Preparing themselves for the realities of the Western Front, men crisscrossed the terrain digging trenches and foxholes while experimenting with barbed wire entanglements.

The ever-patriotic social elite of Menlo Park joined the war effort. Some opened their gardens for the weekend and holiday entertainment of soldiers. Women gathered to make bandages and knit scarves and gloves. Many volunteered their services as drivers or joined the Red Cross. Not uncommonly, flower gardens were planted in vegetables.

East of town, along Willow Road, preparing for an expected influx of military wounded, construction crews erected a sprawling Army hospital complex. At first considered good duty for Army medical personnel, by late summer 1918, with the appearance of deadly Spanish influenza at Camp Fremont, the base hospital was transformed into the scene of unmitigated horror. Hourly, ambulances arrived filled with sick and dying soldiers. Wards became crammed. As the contagion spread,

The town's social elite spearheaded the war effort on the home front.

doctors and nurses succumbed as well. The Army frantically appealed to the community for volunteers to care for the sick.

But Camp Fremont was closed immediately following the war in 1919. At least some measure of tranquility returned to Menlo Park.

During the 1920s, the base hospital — by the end of the twentieth century virtually all that remained of early Camp Fremont — was taken over, modernized and maintained as a hospital by the Veterans Administration.

In 1923, the town's social elite seceded to form the newly created incorporated town of Atherton. Menlo Park, now minus the great estates, voted to incorporate on its own in 1927. For a decade, town fathers wrestled with the difficulties of making their new government function smoothly.

Other events became indelibly etched in the memories of residents. Many vividly remember the widening of El Camino Real between 1937 and 1940 as one of the pivotal events of Menlo Park's modern era. For a time, designated as U.S. Highway 101, graveled El Camino Real was paved and widened from two lanes to four. Old buildings crowding the roadway along the west side of the street were either destroyed or physically moved back to create necessary space.

This civic improvement became something of a historical bench mark. For at least two generations after 1940, residents recalling events of that period, commonly referred to them as having occurred "just before" or "just after" the widening.

Yet another pivotal development in the growth of Menlo Park came during the 1940s. The Army again played a decisive role in the town's history. In 1943, anticipating a tremendous influx of wounded soldiers from the Pacific Theater of operations, historic *Sherwood Hall*, the Barron-Latham-Hopkins estate between El Camino and Middlefield Road, was acquired by the government.

The palatial house was dismantled and the sprawling 94-unit, Dibble General Hospital, each building connected to the other by miles of corridors, was erected in its place. By 1944, Dibble was transformed into a specialty hospital. It became a center for the treatment of blinded soldiers and those requiring surgical reconstruction. Many townsfolk volunteered to assist in the hospital.

Fifty years after Dibble closed, longtime Menlo Park residents still painfully remembered bandaged and blinded veterans, often without limbs or otherwise

Belle Haven homes, built in the 1930s when this photograph was taken, boomed again during the post-World War II era.

grotesquely scarred, walking the streets of the community, again learning how to function. Military authorities requested that townsfolk not interfere with this essential training by attempting to assist even those who appeared confused or in need.

Following the closure of Dibble, when returning veterans created a crush of new students, many former hospital buildings were used by Stanford University to provide housing for married students.

In 1947, after almost 20 years of planning, Stanford Research Institute was established in the same buildings.

And the next year, Menlo Park Mayor Charles P. Burgess managed to arrange for the purchase of 26 acres of the one-time hospital property for ultimate use as a new civic center. Many of the old military buildings were used to house city offices.

Perhaps no single event so thoroughly altered historical patterns in the town of Menlo Park as the creation and growth of Silicon Valley, which began in the final decades of the twentieth century. Property values have skyrocketed as this new affluent population converged on the town.

Through it all, though the town has managed to maintain its quaintness and bucolic environment, it has in fact carved itself a significant niche in the history of the West.

This is Menlo Park.

San Francisquito Creek marks the dividing line between San Mateo and Santa Clara counties. El Palo Alto, a towering coast redwood, is the site where Spanish explorers camped in 1769.

②SAN FRANCISQUITO CREEK

When enough rain falls, water pushes over the top of Searsville Lake dam and begins winding on a 13-mile trek through Stanford University, Menlo Park and Palo Alto, ultimately pouring into the bay at East Palo Alto.

This is San Francisquito Creek, a natural boundary dividing San Mateo and Santa Clara counties. As early as 1777, Franciscan padres, who named the waterway, designated the creek as the dividing line between San Francisco Mission and Santa Clara Mission lands. It is one of the Bay Area's few remaining natural waterways and the South Bay's last steelhead run. It is the largest natural creek on the Peninsula that snakes through a heavily populated area.

The San Francisquito's watershed is 24,320 acres. The communities which drain into it include Woodside, Portola Valley, Ladera and unincorporated parts of San Mateo County. During the winter, the creek can be flush and turbulent; in summer, it is dry.

Creek banks have long been considered an Ohlone Indian archeological site. In 1920, 1950 and 1998, erosion has yielded bones, revealing that Native Americans had been buried along the creek somewhere between 500 and 15,000 years ago.

Rancho de las Pulgas, *comprising 35,240 acres, extended south from San Mateo Creek as far as San Francisquito Creek. It was the Peninsula's largest land grant.*

RANCHO DE LAS PULGAS

In the days of the Spanish missionaries, land along the banks of San Francisquito Creek was used for the herding of sheep; crops were not grown there.

Allegedly as early as 1795, California Governor Diego de Borica, in return for loyal service, had granted 69,000 Peninsula acres to José Argüello, then commandant of the San Francisco Presidio.

But documentation for this claim was lacking. A legitimate, albeit reduced amount of land, was granted to Luís Argüello, son of the commandant, in 1820. This became *Rancho de las Pulgas* (Ranch of the Fleas), a name originally used by Spanish soldiers of the Gaspar de Portolá expedition (1769) after having spent a night in a flea-infested Indian habitation. The grant, 35,240 acres, extended south from San Mateo Creek, including all of the Peninsula's bay front to San Francisquito Creek, and from the bay west to the ridge of the hills.

Luís Argüello died in 1830, before taking possession of the property. Five years later, it passed to his widow and numerous children. But Maria Argüello chose not to live there, making her home in the well-to-do Mexican community that had grown up in the environs of Mission Dolores in present-day San Francisco. Not until 1846, when American military forces seized California, did the Argüello family establish residence at the *Rancho*. They visited the modest adobe, located at the base of the hills behind San Carlos, infrequently.

Nevertheless, by 1851, squatters had moved in, notably in the areas of Redwood Slough, Ravenswood and Menlo Park. Although American land commissioners confirmed the Argüello claim, the family ultimately lost most of it paying attorneys and agents responsible for the victory.

The rancho was granted to Don Luís Argüello in 1835. His descendants owned the property until the 1850s. Pictured is José Ramon Argüello, son of Luís.

New Englander I.C. Woods built Woodside Dairy *during the early 1850s. The elegant home became the prototype of fashionable Peninsula living.*

④ I.C. WOODS PIONEERS ELEGANT COUNTRY LIVING

It was in July 1852 that Isaiah Churchill Woods Jr. (1825-1880), a descendant of a New Bedford, Massachusetts, family, acquired 3,673 acres on the Peninsula south of what became Redwood City. There he laid out the village of Ravenswood (a name combining his own and ravens because of the number of huge crows inhabiting the marsh), the first townsite in San Mateo County. Most of that property, bordered by the bay and what is now Middlefield Road, is presently located in what became Menlo Park.

Woods also built a fine home on 80 acres, initiating Menlo Park's development as a region of luxury country estates for wealthy gentlemen. The richly ornamented structure known as *Woodside Dairy* stood on ground later acquired by the Archdiocese of San Francisco for use as St. Patrick's Seminary. *Woodside Dairy*, characterized by broad porches and French windows, was superior to any other home on the Peninsula during the 1850s. It became the site of lavish entertaining and weekend parties. Woods entertained on the same grandiose scale as magnifico William C. Ralston did a decade later in Belmont. Woods transported his guests down the bay by steamship, putting them ashore at Ravenswood pier. Carriages brought them to the home.

I.C. Woods, president of the powerful Adams Banking and Express Company in San Francisco, had been regarded by admirers as a man of vision and one of the ablest business people in California. Even so, the company failed in 1855. Woods was subsequently accused of embezzling $300,000 in gold from company vaults. Though some claimed that the charges were untrue and that Woods was a convenient scapegoat, he fled California for Australia. The dream of Ravenswood faded and the property was sold. *Woodside Dairy* was acquired by Woods' brother-in-law R. Emmett Doyle, brother of Menlo Park attorney John T. Doyle.

Rustic St. Denis, erected in 1853, was the Peninsula's first Roman Catholic Church.

FIRST ROMAN CATHOLIC CHURCH ON PENINSULA

St. Denis Church was dedicated in 1853. Located on the north bank of San Francisquito Creek near the present-day Stanford Linear Accelerator, it was the first Roman Catholic Church built in San Mateo County. The simple redwood structure with arched windows was on the property of pioneer settler Dennis Martin (1821-1890). It was named for Martin's patron saint.

A native of Wexford, Ireland, Martin came to California in 1844 as a member of the Murphy-Stevens party, the first wagon train to cross the Sierra Nevada. He established himself near San Francisquito Creek, where he built a sawmill, becoming the region's first lumberman of note. Martin erected the church for his family, employees and neighbors. Nevertheless, on Sundays, many parishioners came from predominantly Catholic Menlo Park; others made the trek from as far away as Redwood City. Mass was celebrated by Jesuit priests from Mission Santa Clara, who rode there on horseback.

The last service at the original St. Denis was in the early 1870s. St. Denis ceased to function as an active house of worship after the opening of Menlo Park's Church of the Nativity in 1872.

A humble graveyard, associated with St. Denis, held the remains of Menlo Park's Catholic pioneers until 1953 when the cemetery was relocated.

Upon his arrival in California, Atherton found the Mexican capital at Monterey to be primitive and unpleasant.

Faxon Dean Atherton

⑥ FAXON D. ATHERTON

As a young man during the 1830s, Faxon D. Atherton (1815-1877) had established himself as a merchant in Valparaiso, Chile, where he quickly learned the importance of Alta California. Commerce-conscious New Englanders were especially attracted to California because the province offered an apparently unlimited supply of cattle hides then much in demand for the boot and shoe industry of the American Northeast.

Atherton first visited California in 1836, arriving at Monterey in April. He found neither streets nor hotels. The ground was strewn with the bleached bones of cattle, randomly slaughtered exclusively for their hides and tallow. The air was heavy with menacing vultures and squawking crows feasting on rotting carcasses. The stench was overwhelming.

He later wrote: "I know that I have suffered more in California than I ever did in my life before, traveling day after day, crossing mountains under...burning sun, swimming rivers, sleeping night after night in the open air...expecting each moment to be bit by a rattlesnake, scalped by an Indian, used up by a panther or grizzly bear...." Upon returning to Chile he added that he'd been sickened by California, a vile and miserable land inhabited by villainous scoundrels.

Nevertheless, he recognized California's financial advantages. In 1839 he declared, that if it were ever acquired by the Americans, he would build a home on the Peninsula south of San Francisco.

Long before moving to California, Atherton was profiting from an important Pacific commercial network that included this isolated Mexican province. Through an agent he began acquiring large tracts of California real estate. Thus by the time Atherton arrived in California in 1859, he had already achieved significant local social rank.

Social life at Menlo Park during the 1880s often centered around polite veranda conversation. Pictured at Valparaiso Park is much of the local aristocracy. Left to right (standing) are Mrs. Christian de Guigné, Miss Selby, Mrs. Hayne, Mrs. Pinckard (with Eyre), Mrs. John Parrott II, Miss Jennie Flood, Mrs. Agnes Poett Howard, Mrs. Girvin and son Dick. Seated are Miss Daisy Casserly and Miss Christine Parrott (later Mrs. Joseph Donohoe II).

⑦ ATHERTON FAMILY WAS NUCLEUS OF LOCAL HIGH SOCIETY

Valparaiso Park

Among the first of the exquisite estates to be erected in Menlo Park was *Valparaiso Park*, completed in 1861 for millionaire Faxon D. Atherton. This stately wooden home, uniting the architectural styles of New England with the type of houses Atherton had come to know while living in Valparaiso, Chile, had fourteen-foot ceilings and wide verandas, built on one square mile of land at the southern end of the former *Rancho de las Pulgas*. The estate had formal Victorian gardens characterized by low-clipped boxwood hedges along pathways.

Atherton spent his early professional years in Valparaiso, Chile, where he achieved the status of a merchant prince. Further elevating his station, he married Dominga de Goñi, daughter of a Spanish aristocratic family. The couple became parents of seven children, six of whom were born in Chile.

The soft-spoken and apparently intellectual Atherton moved his family to San Francisco in the latter years of the California Gold Rush, initially making his home on fashionable Rincon Hill while building on the Peninsula.

Valparaiso Park became a center of Peninsula leisure society. Atherton children inter-married with other local well-to-do families, notably the Selbys, Eyres and Macondrays. These bonds, often amounting to familial alliances, formed the basis of a powerful local aristocracy.

The Athertons were Catholic, conservative, and eminently correct. The family head was a stereotypical country gentleman.

Tracks of the San Francisco & San Jose Railroad reached Menlo Park in 1863. The line ushered in an era of prosperity for the community.

TRACKS ALONG THE PENINSULA

Even before 1850, when the California capital was located briefly in San Jose, stagecoach travel had been instituted along the Peninsula. The trip was both long and expensive and, as a result, few outsiders were seen in Menlo Park before a railroad reached the little hamlet.

Construction work on the San Francisco & San Jose Railroad finally began in spring of 1861. Materials for the line were brought by ship from the American East, along a circuitous water route around Cape Horn. Though delayed by the beginning of the Civil War, track laying was well under way by the beginning of 1863.

In September of that year, tracks reached Menlo Park, which for a brief time marked the end of the line. The first regular train between San Francisco and Menlo Park, in October, hit a horse. Thereafter, most daily trips were uneventful, except that farmers along the route complained about sparks from the engines igniting numerous grass fires.

Service to San Jose was completed by early 1864. The line was opened with appropriate celebration January 16. For business and pleasure, people thronged the line. In a single month, April 1864, the train carried 16,925 passengers. Freight figures were equally impressive. For the same month, they included 100 tons of grain, 21,000 pounds of charcoal, 500 cords of firewood, 20,000 dozen eggs, 1,000 pigs, fruit, hides and a list of other products.

A passenger train crossing San Francisquito Creek at Menlo Park, 1863.

⑨ Gala picnic at San Francisquito Creek, 1863

By 1863, a decade-long dream of rail service along the Peninsula had almost been realized. Coming rapidly to a close was the colorful era of stagecoach travel when, on good days, it took only nine hours to ride between San Jose and San Francisco.

A ceremonial groundbreaking for a Peninsula railroad had been staged at San Francisquito Creek, dividing line between Santa Clara and San Mateo counties, May 1, 1861. Now, October 17, 1863, California Governor Leland Stanford stood at the same spot to preside over a celebration marking the successful laying of 35 miles of track from San Francisco to Mayfield. Menlo Park could now be reached in 80 minutes.

An excursion train brought 400 revelers for a gigantic picnic. Participants viewed this short stretch of rail as a symbolic first link in a great transcontinental railroad that they hoped would ultimately unite the Atlantic and the Pacific.

The train, consisting of six passenger coaches and a number of freight cars, ran smoothly to Mayfield. Then it backed up to the creek for the picnic.

No expense had been spared providing victuals for the guests. There were turkey, chicken, ham, beef, bread, pickles and sauerkraut. Champagne and other wines flowed freely.

Rail operations between San Francisco and Mayfield began October 18, 1863. Service to San Jose was not completed until early the next year.

Railroad baron Leland Stanford marked the arrival of the tracks at Menlo Park by hosting a gala picnic.

George C. Johnson

Timothy Guy Phelps

Faxon D. Atherton

Leander Ransome made the initial survey of what became the town of Menlo Park.

Simon M. Mezes acquired much of Rancho de las Pulgas *from the Argüello family after the Land Act of 1851. He became a director of the Menlo Park Villa Association.*

⑩Menlo Park Villa Association

In March 1863, with the promise that the railroad would soon reach San Francisquito Creek, the Menlo Park Villa Association was formed by leading landowners of the region.

A tract, comprising 1,500 acres of former *Rancho de las Pulgas* land, extending both east and west of the still unfinished tracks, was laid out by surveyor Leander Ransom. It made up a large portion of what became the town of Menlo Park.

Investors in this real estate promotion offered lots for sale to those desiring to build country homes. Buyers were assured that this portion of the Peninsula was unsurpassed for magnificent weather. Extremes of heat and cold were never felt, and vicious winds and fogs rarely reached into Menlo Park.

Formation of the Villa Association constituted the genesis of a new town. Promoters of the scheme, the ilk of Faxon D. Atherton, capitalist George C. Johnson, Congressman Timothy Guy Phelps, San Francisco industrialist Thomas H. Selby, land speculator Simon M. Mezes, and local landlord Dennis J. Oliver agreed that this section of the Peninsula was renowned for wonderful soil, large and splendid live oaks, and other evergreen shade trees.

Although records indicate that lots sold steadily over the next several years, demand for them was less than backers had hoped. Nevertheless, by 1870, scores of home lots had sold and a small downtown area, along Oak Grove Avenue near the railroad track, had begun to develop.

Menlo Park train depot, a local historical treasure, is considered the oldest surviving station on the Peninsula.

OLDEST TRAIN DEPOT ON PENINSULA

When, in 1970, there was talk of remodeling and perhaps moving the Menlo Park Railroad Station, Leslie Merrill, then executive director of the San Mateo County Historical Association, wrote to the developer, making the Association's policy known. Few letters were ever more succinct. "Touch that [the Menlo Park station] and you die," wrote Merrill.

Not only was Menlo Park station the oldest train depot on the Peninsula, it was thought to be the oldest such structure in California. A primitive shed-like building erected in 1863 and located on the northwest side of the present Oak Grove Avenue, it served as the town's original station. By 1867, the town already needed a more sophisticated facility. Thus, the 1863 shed was loaded on a flat car and moved north to the tiny hamlet of Belmont where it became *that* town's first station.

An extremely functional but substantial new Menlo Park depot, a three-room building constructed of redwood, was built. One room served as the station master's office. There were separate waiting rooms for men and women.

The structure was enlarged and made more ornate in the early 1890s. Decorative elements, primarily Victorian-Gothic and Queen Anne styled, were added along with ornate furnishing and adornments in the ladies waiting room. At that time, an additional small waiting room was appended to the depot. This room was for the exclusive use of Mrs. Leland Stanford.

Thomas Selby (left) is seated with his family on the porch at Almendral.

②LORD OF ALMENDRAL

"A man of uncommon breeding" is what people called Thomas H. Selby (1820-1873), who acquired 480 acres in the Fair Oaks section of Menlo Park in 1863. The estate was called *Almendral*.

This summer retreat was characterized by rich foliage and broad fields of waving grain. Selby raised cattle and produced 10,000 bushels of grain annually. He also maintained the Peninsula's largest fruit orchard. Selby's home was known for its antique furnishings and paintings, most of which were imported from England.

Few Menlo Park pioneers boasted such a distinguished pedigree. For hundreds of years, the family had figured in English military and naval annals. Selbys had served in Parliament, sat on the English bench, and been clergymen in the Church of England. The family still owned estates in Britain dating from the reign of Edward I. In the medieval town of York, in 1069, William the Conqueror had founded Selby Abbey. The family name is still found among the memorial tablets in Westminster Abbey.

The American Selbys established themselves in Maryland during the seventeenth century and by the time of the War for Independence had achieved political prominence.

In California, Selby became a Gold Rush merchant. But his fortune was based in lead. He created the Selby Smelting and Lead Works in 1856, becoming the first to build a large-scale smelting works in the West. By 1870, ore from every state and territory west of the Rockies was sent to Selby's plant for smelting.

Strict and elitist, the Selbys became notable members of the emerging Peninsula aristocracy. Thomas Selby's daughter Jennie married Faxon Atherton Jr. Son Percy Selby went to the altar with Elena Atherton. Another daughter married Andrew Jackson Ralston, brother of the Bank of California founder.

Thomas H. Selby

⑬ PENINSULA HIGH SOCIETY'S SOUTHERN FLAIR

Thomas H. Selby had a thoroughly regal persona. A torchlight procession of more than a thousand San Franciscans paraded to his Rincon Hill home in September 1869 to applaud him following his election as the city's thirteenth mayor.

If any single family helped rescue frontier San Francisco from social doldrums and its reputation as a crude gold camp, it was the Selbys. Thomas Selby built one of the earliest great houses on exclusive Rincon Hill. The house contained San Francisco's original ballroom. Social commentators found Selby's wife remarkable. She was the former Henrietta Reese from a prominent Alabama family. Scribes noted that she was a fragile little lady but "indefatigable in hospitality." She entertained constantly, both in San Francisco and at their Menlo Park retreat. *Almendral* was famed for elaborate gardens, its iron gate and the Peninsula's first spouting fountain.

Mrs. Selby inaugurated a warm social regime, decidedly Southern in conviviality and distinction. Her easy grace, a style that most wives of bonanza kings never managed to duplicate, gradually became regarded as Old San Francisco and Peninsula tradition. Social events at the Selbys were eagerly attended. Mrs. Selby delighted planning 17-course dinners. She once commented that guests were seated by six o'clock and, if anyone got up before midnight, she considered the evening a failure.

*A highlight of **Almendral** was the Peninsula's first spouting fountain. A photograph around the fountain became a tradition when visiting the Selbys. Included in the photo are the Selbys, Athertons, Macondrays and the Andrew Jackson Ralstons. These families all were related by marriage.*

Menlo Park pioneer William E. Barron had made his fortune as an owner of the New Almaden Quicksilver Mine near Los Gatos. It was the most valuable mining property in California.

WILLIAM E. BARRON — MILTON LATHAM ESTATE

By the 1860s, Menlo Park was already becoming known for large and luxurious homes usually surrounded by acres of lushly landscaped grounds. Among the most celebrated of the homes built east of the railroad tracks was a towered Victorian belonging to William E. Barron, one of the Peninsula's first British pioneers. Barron had been an owner of the incredibly rich New Almaden Quicksilver Mine near Los Gatos. He was also San Francisco representative of the powerful international firm of Barron & Forbes.

Two months after his death in October 1871, executors of his estate sold the 380-acre Menlo Park property for $75,000. The buyer was former U.S. Senator Milton S. Latham.

Despite the mansion's elegance, it wasn't *new*, and Latham declared that one day he would raze it to build something more distinguished. Meanwhile, however, he was eager to move in. Contractors were dispatched to Menlo Park to put the house in suitably habitable condition.

The entire house underwent refitting, repainting and redecorating. Amid this frenzy of activity, the impatient Latham ordered workers to combat dampness by burning oil stoves day and night to dry paint and wallpaper. Fires were set in fireplaces and glowing coals pulled out on hearths to exude more heat. Perhaps not surprisingly, the building was set ablaze and burned to the foundation. The house and its furnishings had been fully insured; Latham's men immediately set to work building a virtual castle.

Johnson's daughter-in-law Kate is seated on the porch of Heart's Ease *(formerly known as* Woodside Dairy*).*

15 MENLO PARK'S NORWEGIAN PIONEER

Norwegian George C. Johnson, a major landowner in Menlo Park, was also the consul general for Norway and Sweden.

Genial George C. Johnson, a one-time sea captain from Bergen, Norway, who arrived in California during the Gold Rush, became a real estate speculator and owner of the most important steel importing firm on the Pacific Coast.

A resident of San Francisco's South Park and consul general of Norway and Sweden, he began acquiring extensive Menlo Park properties during the 1850s, purchasing the land of pioneer Dennis J. Oliver. Subsequent Peninsula acquisitions, including most of Ravenswood, transformed Johnson into one of the largest landowners in the area.

Upon his demise in 1872, Johnson properties passed to his son Robert C. Johnson and daughter-in-law Kate (1834-1893). Fond of the isolation and tranquility of Menlo Park, Kate Johnson, vacationed on the Peninsula at *Woodside Dairy*, one-time estate of I.C. Woods. She renamed the sprawling vine-covered house *Heart's Ease*. Mrs. Johnson, a Presbyterian, who had abandoned a husband and daughter in Michigan before coming to California in 1861, became increasingly reclusive. Finally, in 1878, she converted to Roman Catholicism.

Robert Johnson died in 1889. Kate was soon a favorite acquaintance of San Francisco Archbishop Patrick William Riordan, to whom she ultimately bequeathed a third of her vast fortune. Kate Johnson was California's largest contributor to the Catholic Church during the 1890s. Among other generous gifts, she bequeathed *Heart's Ease* to the church. This is the property on which St. Patrick's Seminary was erected in 1898.

The house burned to the ground in July 1909.

James T. Watkins became the commodore of the Pacific Mail Steamship Company and, as such, commanded the first trans-Pacific voyages between San Francisco and the Orient.

16 PACIFIC MAIL STEAMSHIP'S COMMODORE WAS TRUE LOCAL LEGEND

James Thomas Watkins (1808-1867) was a seafaring man. Annapolis-born, he had gone to sea at age 12 and was a captain before his twenty-first birthday. His initial circuit of Cape Horn was in 1832 and his first trans-Pacific voyage in 1839.

By the advent of the Gold Rush, he'd settled in San Francisco, in the employ of the powerful Pacific Mail Steamship Company. He commanded the *Panama*, one of the original side-wheel steamers to reach San Francisco. His home was in South Park.

Impressed by his maritime skill, the company sent Watkins east to supervise construction of the new three-deck steamship *San Francisco*, heralded as the finest steamship afloat.

With Watkins as its skipper, bound for California, the *San Francisco* sailed from New York December 22, 1853, with 800 passengers, including 600 soldiers. The voyage was ill-fated. Two days out, in the eye of a gale, waves swept across the ship, splintering her cabin and washing 150 passengers overboard. The ship was lost.

This tragedy didn't damage his career. He later commanded the steamers *Golden Gate, Golden Age,* and *Constitution.* And in 1855, he was elevated to the coveted position of commodore. As such he took the helm of the *Colorado,* the first steamship to inaugurate regular Pacific crossings between San Francisco, Hong Kong, and Tokyo.

On the moonless night of November 12, 1867, Watkins was skippering the Pacific Mail steamer *Costa Rica* en route from Nagasaki to Shanghai. The commodore tripped while walking the deck, tumbled through an open hatch cover, and fell into the ship's cavernous hold. He succumbed to a cerebral hemorrhage caused by the fall.

Commodore Watkins ordered construction of Fair Oaks *in Menlo Park.*

FAIR OAKS WAS ONE OF EARLIEST HOMES

The Watkins family was photographed at the Menlo Park home. The commodore died before Fair Oaks *was completed.*

Shortly after the completion of the Peninsula railroad in 1864, James T. Watkins, Commodore of the Pacific Mail Steamship Company, sought a piece of property in Menlo Park. In 1866, he purchased 20 acres adjacent to the main gate of Faxon D. Atherton's *Valparaiso Park.* Ship carpenters constructed a steep-roofed, 3,500 square foot Gothic Revival house which became a landmark of the area. Impressed by the number of oaks highlighting the region, Watkins called the house *Fair Oaks* (the name that was also given to the local train stop). Watkins referred to the estate simply as "the Farm." The land was planted in fruit trees.

According to legend, Watkins had the house built in Connecticut, prefabricated and shipped around Cape Horn as ballast. A romantic tale, but historical evidence of it is lacking. In 1903, however, when the house was moved from its original location on Isabella Avenue, workers noting the hardwood used in construction, hypothesized that at least the beams had been imported from the East.

Watkins died before the home was completed; he never lived there. After Watkins' demise, his widow sold the South Park home and moved to *Fair Oaks.*

Although slated for destruction during the 1990s, the house was again moved from Isabella to a new location, in Atherton, along Alejandra Avenue near Menlo College.

*Built in 1868, Unadilla was
the country estate of the
William James Adams family.*

William James Adams

Cassandra Hills Adams

WILLIAM JAMES ADAMS

The stately old Menlo Park house with its extensive grounds, built in 1868, was called *Unadilla*. This was the home of Mr. and Mrs. William James Adams and their trio of daughters.

The family, of Scots heritage originally from Northern Ireland, had settled in New England during the eighteenth century. William James Adams (1835-1907) came west during the Gold Rush, establishing a grocery business in Sacramento and San Francisco. His first fortune was lost when his primary place of business was wiped out in one of the many San Francisco fires of the 1850s. Thereafter, recognizing San Francisco's ongoing need for lumber, he went into that business, calling it Adams & Blinn and subsequently the Washington Mill Company. Adams acquired lumber mills on Puget Sound and in the state of Mississippi. He came to own 27 lumber schooners. On the Peninsula, he was an original trustee of Menlo Park, having been elected in 1874 during the town's brief incorporation and helped build the Episcopal Parish of the Holy Trinity.

Unadilla was built close enough to the rail line that the train's mournful whistle could be clearly heard in the drawing rooms. It was typical of country houses of that era. Wide steps led from manicured lawns to an especially broad awning-shaded veranda furnished with rocking chairs.

The interior was characterized by spacious rooms with heavy Victorian furniture. Oil paintings decorated the walls. On the first floor were the parlor, a sitting room, dining room, and smoking room in addition to the kitchen and pantry. Upstairs were numerous sleeping chambers all furnished in mahogany. Chests of drawers were topped in marble.

Curving stairs led to a tower, allowing occupants to look over the tops of surrounding ivy-skirted oaks and see as far east as the marshes leading to San Francisco Bay. Adams' grandson, Ansel, who became the famed twentieth-century photographer, wrote that he enjoyed quiet reading in the room atop the tower.

The grounds, described as "an immense piece of tapestry work," were considered second only to Leland Stanford's in elegance. The house burned in 1908.

Elmwood became the home of Charles Holbrook.

⑲ CHARLES HOLBROOK SOUGHT A HEALTHFUL CLIMATE

Finding himself in poor health in 1880, Charles Holbrook (1830-1925), a partner in the San Francisco merchant firm of Holbrook, Merrill & Stetson, decided he wanted to live in the country. The Menlo Park station agent convinced him that there was probably no more healthful area in the world.

Of English heritage whose family came to American in 1643, Holbrook purchased an existing six-year-old house along Watkins Avenue. He named the eight-bedroom residence *Elmwood*. It became Holbrook's summer retreat and supplied his family year-round supplies of fresh fruits, vegetables, meat and dairy products. Not long after acquiring the Menlo Park home, Holbrook recovered his health. Late in his life, he credited relaxing summers on the Peninsula for his 95 years.

Its owner credited Elmwood's Eden-like existence for his longevity.

He personally laid out the grounds. Seventeen acres were in hay, one in orchard, half an acre in vegetables, berries and grapes. There were apples, pears, and figs. Surrounding the house were three acres of lawns and colorful flower borders. Appropriately, half an acre was planted in elm trees to shield the house from the road.

Holbrook's daughter Olive (1878-1958) married Silas H. Palmer (1875-1963) at *Elmwood*, spring 1903. A special train brought 250 guests from San Francisco for the happy occasion. She bequeathed the house and 22 acres to the town of Atherton for use as a public park.

Charles Holbrook

Rincon Hill in San Francisco was the center of local high society. All viewed Milton Latham's home as the hill's most luxurious.

Latham's neighbors fully expected him to be the first Westerner to occupy the White House.

㉒ EASTERNER WITH SOUTHERN CIVILITY

Tremendous excitement prevailed in Menlo Park in 1871 when Milton S. Latham (1827-1882) purchased the William E. Barron estate. Men were amazed by his political dexterity and expected one day to see him in the White House. Latham, an attorney who came to California in 1850, was elected to Congress in 1853. Six years later, at the age of 29, he'd been elected governor. But two days after his inauguration the following January, upon being chosen as a U.S. Senator by the legislature to complete the unfinished term of Senator David Broderick, Latham resigned. He became the youngest person yet to serve in the Senate.

A suave Easterner, raised in Alabama, Latham prided himself on being a gentleman. Uncomfortable with the Senate's vulgarity, he found that a single term was enough. After a sojourn in Europe attempting to recover his gentility, Latham returned to California to manage the London and San Francisco Bank.

During the 1870s, while building the Menlo Park estate, he became a dominant force in Northern California railroading, acquiring control of the North Pacific Coast Railroad, a narrow gauge line which followed a circuitous route from Sausalito to Cazadero on the Russian River. Eventually railroading broke Latham's financial back. He resigned from the bank in 1878. Furniture and possessions from his enormous Rincon Hill house were sold at auction. Auctioneers began selling off his Menlo Park estate in September 1880.

Thereafter, Latham went east to assume the presidency of the New York Mining Exchange.

Neighbors acclaimed Milton Latham's Menlo Park estate for its majesty and elegance.

㉑ THURLOW LODGE

Newspaper readers were mesmerized by details of Milton Latham's *Thurlow Lodge*, the 50-room Menlo Park mansion that rose on the foundation of the burned out Barron estate. The curly-haired Latham lavished easily a million dollars on the structure.

Elaborately carved and corniced, the house was immense with a tower rising just over 98 feet above the ground. On the house's southern front was a veranda 16 feet in depth. Rooms were soon crammed with sculpture, paintings and objects of art gathered in Europe. Readers cooed over progress reports. One told of the installation of a hydraulic elevator and another of two full-grown palm trees purchased from the town of San Jose. The grounds, a picture of floral art, were graced at every turn by fountains along with marble and bronze statuary in the form of foxes, lions, dogs, bears, winged beasts, and horses. Manicured gardens were surrounded by a natural park of oaks.

In addition to the grand house, Latham erected an ornate one-story barn with a mansard roof. The entrance, marked by a full-sized horse head in bronze, was surmounted by a clocked belfry, where a 300-pound bell was faithfully rung on the hour.

Latham's collection included 32 carriages with a matching pair of horses for each. Carriage, stable, and harness rooms were done in varnished redwood and cedar.

Joseph A. Donohoe with family (beneath the tree) survey **Holm Grove,** *their Peninsula sanctuary. Menlo-Atherton High School is presently on this site.*

Joseph A. Donohoe

Emilie Blain Donohoe

JOSEPH A. DONOHOE

Modest though he may have been, no banker in early San Francisco was more revered or more genuinely respected than Joseph A. Donohoe (1826-1895). Throughout the course of a long banking career, he assiduously avoided the limelight.

Donohoe maintained a richly appointed town house, built in 1862 on Rincon Hill. Six years later he acquired *Holm Grove*, 40 acres on the east side of Middlefield Road in Menlo Park, where he built a stately three-story Victorian, filling it with sumptuous furnishings.

A Roman Catholic, Donohoe had a chapel built into one room. There was an automatic elevator which worked by water pressure. His household, in 1870, included five servants and a coachman. This property later became part of Menlo-Atherton High School.

In the uncertain world of San Francisco banking, Donohoe always had been known as the city's "safe banker." In December 1860, his firm, Donohoe & Kelly joined with the banking house of Fretz & Ralston. But the ever-cautious Donohoe soon became dissatisfied with what he felt to be unwise loans of partner William C. Ralston. By early 1864, Ralston was secretly planning to open the new Bank of California. This was accomplished in June of that year, and his association with Donohoe was dissolved. The two became arch-competitors.

Donohoe & Kelly were unaffected by the financial panic which resulted in the August 1875 collapse of the Bank of California. The aftermath of that event was the alleged suicide of Ralston. By the end of the year, the firm of Donohoe & Kelly was acclaimed as the most stable in the city and recognized as the leading banking institution in the state.

Donohoe's family became part of the Peninsula's emerging social aristocracy. Two of his children married offspring of John Parrott of San Francisco and San Mateo. His daughter Mary Emilie went to the altar with John Parrott II (1882) and Joseph A. Donohoe II was wed to Noelie Christine Parrott (1888).

Ringwood, *along Middlefield Road, was the oak-studded estate of San Francisco attorney John T. Doyle.*

JOHN T. DOYLE

Mr. and Mrs. John T. Doyle sat for a portrait with their grandchildren.

Perhaps no California lawyer was as respected as John T. Doyle (1819-1906) who built *Ringwood*, a sprawling, two-story, wood frame Menlo Park house in 1868. It was set on 400 oak-studded acres. Neighbors enjoyed gathering on *Ringwood's* wisteria-hung veranda to appreciate Doyle's intellectual Irish wit and conversation. Doyle, visited frequently by neighbor Gertrude Atherton, who admired his book collection, was reputed to have owned one of the best personal libraries in the state.

In 1853, San Francisco Archbishop Joseph S. Alemany presented Doyle with a puzzle that became his passion for half a century. It involved what was called the "Pious Fund of the Californias." The Fund dated from the 1690s when the Spanish king ordered construction of mission settlements in Baja and later Alta California.

At that time, to support the missions, Jesuit priests set out to collect donations from wealthy aristocrats in Old and New Spain. Ultimately amounting to millions, this became known as the Pious Fund. Its provisions were emphatic. Revenues were "solely for the benefit of missions in California."

After California was acquired by the United States in 1848, Pious Fund payments from Mexico ceased. At Alemany's behest, Doyle set out to recover the money. He embarked on an exhaustive personal detective search for information in Spain and Mexico. In 1870, he presented his case to the Mixed American and Mexican Claims Commission in Washington, D.C. This group found in favor of Doyle and the California church. The finding covered California's claims through the year 1869. In the next 20 years, almost a million dollars in Mexican gold were paid to the Catholic Church of California.

Then payments ceased. Doyle, in 1902, sued Mexico in the Permanent Court of Arbitration at The Hague. It was the first controversy brought before that court. Mexico was ordered to pay California an additional $1.5 million.

Menlo Park Hotel became the town's most renowned oasis of rustication.

Martin Kuck (1911)

㉔ AN OASIS OF COMFORT

For decades, Menlo Park Hotel, a fine two-story building dating from February 1868, located near the railroad tracks north of Oak Grove Avenue, was the town's most revered lodging place for travelers.

Proprietors Martin and Diedrich (1830-1876) Kuck, natives of Germany, took pride in their fine rooms with ornate overstuffed furnishings. The hotel could accommodate large numbers of guests. Their "substantial table" was always supplied with all the luxuries the markets could provide.

On the first floor, the brothers maintained a general store offering groceries, hardware, crockery, glassware, and mens' and boys' clothing, in addition to a variety of tobacco products, wines and liquors. This is believed to have been the town's first store.

The showplace grounds won applause for their colorful flower gardens. The property was punctuated with oaks and laurels that adequately shaded tastefully laid out pathways and avenues winding through the grounds. The walks were paved with crushed shells and gardens were ideal for picnics away from the crowded city. There was also a large platform for dancing.

Added attractions for weekend guests included a bowling alley, billiard tables, and a selection of fine liquors and cigars at the bar. A stable, also on the property, provided horses and carriages for excursions to any destination in the area.

CHARLES N. FELTON

(25)

Millionaire Charles Norton Felton (1828-1914) became a resident of Menlo Park in the 1870s. His two-story, pink-frescoed, vine-covered mansion situated on 35 acres almost hidden from view by a forest of trees and bushes on the north side of Encinal Avenue near the tracks, was called *Felton Gables*.

This home became the scene of some of the truly posh entertainments of the nineteenth century. Three presidents, Rutherford B. Hayes, Benjamin Harrison, and Ulysses S. Grant took refreshment in Felton's lavish drawing room.

Distinguished U.S. Senator Charles N. Felton sat with his granddaughter, Marie Louise Elkins. She later married Christian de Guigné Jr.

Felton had come to California as a prospector in 1849. At the time, his total fortune, he said later, amounted to seven silver dimes. In the Mother Lode, he opened a mercantile business and within a few months accumulated $3,000, almost exclusively from the sale of pickles. But the true source of his wealth was from the Comstock Lode. With associate William C. Ralston, Felton invested early. He eventually sold his holdings, realizing a profit of $190,000.

Felton immersed himself in Republican Party politics and served in a variety of positions ranging from treasurer of the U.S. Mint in San Francisco to California State Assemblyman and four years as a member of Congress. He became powerful, although never well-liked. In March 1891, less than a week after the burial of U.S. Senator George Hearst, who died while in office, without enthusiasm and amid charges of political shenanigans, the California legislature elected Felton to the Senate to complete the unfinished term. He left office in 1893 without standing for reelection.

Edward E. Eyre   *Mary Tutt Eyre*

Mr. and Mrs. Edward Eyre sat at the core of Menlo Park high society.

㉖ EDWARD E. EYRE ACCLAIMED AS CIVIL WAR HERO

California Civil War heroes were rare. With the war's outbreak in 1861, the government refused to accept Pacific Coast volunteers because of the expense of transporting them to the war zone. Thus, for Californians, the Civil War was a distant, non-threatening occurrence.

Most federal soldiers stationed in California were transferred East for battlefield service. But hardly had Regulars departed when rebel forces moved into New Mexico and Arizona. This action was interpreted as an effort by the South to establish steppingstones for an invasion of California.

Defense of the Golden State was assigned to the First Regiment of California Volunteer Infantry, later known as the California Column. Lieutenant-Colonel Edward Eyre commanded a battalion-sized advance unit of California cavalry. In summer 1862, the driest in 30 years, his column was ordered to advance through the Southwest into Texas. Eyre's unit left Tucson in June. Horses consumed water-soaked barley and were restricted to a single gallon of water per day. To sustain horses, half of the time men walked dismounted. One canteen of water per day was each man's ration.

The column fought battles with Apache Indians. Many Californians were wounded; a number found scalped and robbed of their uniforms were buried at Apache Pass.

Confederate-held towns in Arizona and New Mexico were recaptured as Southern forces retreated. Eyre's cavalry occupied Fort Thorn on the Rio Grande in Texas, July 4, 1862.

Evaluating the success of the operation, superiors praised Eyre's extraordinary efforts for the Union success in the Southwest. Still, Eyre resigned his commission and returned to San Francisco in November 1862.

Glen-Eyre, *summer resort of the Eyre family, later sold to San Francisco banker Herbert Fleishhacker.*

EDWARD E. EYRE

By the time Edward E. Eyre (1823-1899) retired in 1875, he was respected as the dean of San Francisco's financial community. During the bonanza days of the Nevada Comstock, Eyre, an authority on mining properties, handled the entire stock portfolios of silver titans James C. Flood and partner William O'Brien. At one point, he served as president of the San Francisco Stock Exchange.

Upon retirement, Eyre acquired 40 acres in Menlo Park where he supervised construction of a three-story, 31-room, ornate white Victorian on the east side of County Road not far from Fair Oaks station. His property spread east to the railroad tracks.

Glen-Eyre became a hospitality center. Personages the likes of U.S. Supreme Court Justice Oliver Wendell Holmes, former Secretary of State William Seward, Professor Louis Agassiz as well as writers Richard Henry Dana and Bayard Taylor were entertained there.

For the Eyre family — in addition to the financier and his wife there were six children — Menlo Park was always a summer place. Nevertheless, their arrival lent stature to the increasingly exclusive community. Devout Episcopalians, the Eyres were the major impetus behind construction of the Parish of the Holy Trinity in 1886. Eyre children intermarried with other prominent Menlo Park families, contributing to the growth of a Peninsula aristocracy. His son, Edward L. Eyre, who married Florence Atherton, became the first mayor of Atherton when the town was created in 1923.

During the 1920s, Edward L. Eyre, son of the financier, became the first mayor of Atherton.

Workers built Menlo Park's Church of the Nativity in 1872. The original structure still stands on Oak Grove Avenue.

CHURCH OF THE NATIVITY

Although increasing numbers of Roman Catholics began congregating in Menlo Park during the 1860s, no church was built in town until 1872, when St. Bridget's was erected on Middlefield Road at Ringwood Avenue.

Legal haggling over title to the property necessitated relocation of the church. The small Gothic Revival structure, along with its 120-foot spire, was first dragged to a temporary location on Santa Cruz Avenue (1877), west of County Road. The next year it was again moved to a permanent three-acre lot on Oak Grove Avenue.

Helping to ensure the church's permanence, in 1887, it was lifted on blocks and a brick foundation was placed beneath. At that time, a new nave was added. Additionally, a 1,200-pound bell, a gift of San Francisco industrialist Peter Donahue, was hung in the belfry.

The following year when the white 62 x 137-foot structure was consecrated, the name was changed to Church of the Nativity. Architecturally, it reflected the prevailing tastes of Catholics of that era. Many of the same Gothic Revival characteristics are seen in some of the neighboring residences, most notably *Fair Oaks*, the home built by James T. Watkins. Because of the steadfast determination of parishioners to preserve the historical integrity of the classic structure, few changes have been made in it since 1888.

The silver candlesticks and crucifix made originally for St. Denis Church eventually came to adorn the altar of Church of the Nativity.

(29) INTERIOR DECORATION AT CHURCH OF THE NATIVITY

St. Denis, the area's original Roman Catholic Church, located in the hills west of town, had been erected in 1852 by pioneer lumberman Dennis Martin. A rustic exterior camouflaged the elegance of the interior. Martin commissioned French artisans to fashion an ornate silver crucifix and six silver candlesticks to adorn the altar.

In 1872, when St. Denis was abandoned as a house of worship, all vestments, pews, and most church decoration were given to Menlo Park's Church of the Nativity. The silver crucifix and candlesticks, on the other hand, were taken by parishioner Christine Parrott Donohoe, wife of banker Joseph Donohoe II, to adorn the Donohoe family altar chapel at *Holm Grove*. Years later the Donohoes gave these cherished treasures to the Church of the Nativity, where they went on permanent altar display and are revered as the church's most valued heirlooms.

The interior of the Church of the Nativity is revered for its well-preserved historic ambiance.

There were several boarding houses in the community when the town incorporated in 1874.

③ⓑ COUNTY'S SECOND INCORPORATED TOWN

There were major problems with drainage and local residents were dissatisfied with the condition of town streets. In an effort to creatively deal with the problems, March 23, 1874, Menlo Park citizens voted to incorporate.

The town became the county's second incorporated entity. Boundaries were drawn to include most of present-day Atherton and east to the bay absorbing all of old Ravenswood. According to Menlo Park's new charter the town was to be administered by five elected trustees: L.P. Cooley, John T. Doyle, George C. Broadman, Charles N. Felton and William James Adams.

Almost immediately trustees purchased 1,500 cubic yards of gravel and work crews went to work surfacing Middlefield Road. Additionally, in April, a volunteer fire department was organized. When necessary improvements had been completed, trustees ceased to meet and, in 1876, the incorporation was allowed to lapse.

M. K. SMITH COLLECTION

MURRAY FAMILY WAS ONE OF MANY FROM IRELAND

Irish immigrant John Murray acquired land in Menlo Park during the 1880s. When the property was purchased for the Allied Arts Guild, original structures were disguised and incorporated into the new enterprise.

During Ireland's great potato famine of the 1840s, it is estimated that 750,000 Irishmen died and approximately a million more emigrated to other countries.

One immigrant who arrived in New York in 1848 was John Murray (1825-1894) from a small village in Queens County of central Ireland. While in New York, Murray wed Mary Flynn. The pair headed for California in 1852, settling in Menlo Park to engage in dairy operations. Their principal customer, to whom they supplied butter, was the Pacific Mail Steamship Company.

After a time, having achieved a degree of prosperity during the 1880s, they purchased 200 acres in what became the University Heights neighborhood of Menlo Park. There they built Stanford Dairy, along with a two-story home and barn.

Murray's barn, built in 1885, and home were acquired by Garfield and Delight Merner in 1929. On this property, the Merners created the Allied Arts Guild. The home was subsequently disguised, giving it the appearance of a Spanish revival structure; the barn, largely unchanged, was put into use by the Allied Arts Guild.

Leland and Jane Stanford's arrival on the Peninsula brought new prestige to Menlo Park. This photograph shows their home, Palo Alto, *the former* Mayfield Grange.

(32) STANFORDS ARRIVE ON THE PENINSULA

The 1876 arrival on the Peninsula of the former governor and transcontinental railroad builder Leland Stanford gave added prestige to the already exclusive community of Menlo Park. Stanford purchased *Mayfield Grange*, once property of San Francisco entrepreneur George Gordon. His farm was on the south side of San Francisquito Creek within sight of Menlo Park. Just a mile from the depot, Stanford called the estate *Palo Alto*.

Stanford's spread was transformed into a genuine Peninsula showplace. The old home, reached via a broad avenue which wound through dense foliage, was modified and enlarged. Surrounding the house were five acres of lawn, rare palms, shrubs and beds of brilliant flowering plants. Nearby were 50 acres of orchards and vineyards.

By 1880, Stanford, who spent much of his time devising novel improvements to the house and grounds, had planted 3,600 specimens of eastern and foreign trees, 300 different species of azaleas and rhododendrons along with 118 varieties of camellias. There were also 1,108 fruit trees of 272 different varieties.

Stanford, who until the establishment of the university was enamored with the town of Menlo Park, believed the climate there to be among the most nearly perfect in the world. He claimed that the enviable weather conditions were shared only with Cape Colony in South Africa and a location in Russia, 200 miles south of Moscow.

Palo Alto *Trotting Stable, the pride of Leland Stanford, acquired international fame and inflated the reputation of Menlo Park.*

(33) STANFORD CREATES HORSE PARADISE

California's most celebrated carrot patch during the 1880s was planted at *Palo Alto.* The 60-acre plot was grown exclusively for Leland Stanford's horses.

Horses were Stanford's passion and always received maximum comfort and consideration. Spacious stalls were kept clean and pleasant smelling and were arranged so horses could see one another. Loud talking and swearing by grooms were strictly forbidden around the horses. Verbal abuse of an animal brought reprimand.

Stanford's farm brought international fame to little-known Menlo Park. Horse-loving visitors from around the world converged. At *Palo Alto,* they found 50 redwood paddocks, two race tracks, a training school and a canopied "kindergarten" for young horses. The farm was a wonder of the equine world.

At all times, Stanford kept 400 mares and anywhere from 20 to 30 stallions. It wasn't uncommon for him to stable as many as 750 horses, each with an illustrious pedigree. It was whispered that to acquire these animals he had decimated the breeding stock of the state of Kentucky. Stanford's was easily the largest such enterprise in the world.

Stanford's horse training techniques, soon known as the "Palo Alto system," were adopted all over the nation. *Palo Alto* horses won a total of 19 international records. By 1891, every world trotting record was held by one of Stanford's animals.

The plebeian origins of the Floods placed them outside the aristocratic inner circle of Menlo Park's better society.

James C. Flood

Mary Emma Flood

34 FLOOD FAMILY WAS GREETED WITH AMBIVALENCE

The arrival of silver tycoon James C. Flood (1826-1889) at Menlo Park in the late 1870s was not a cause for celebration among members of the local social aristocracy. Many sneered at Flood's plebeian origins, viewing him as a "parvenu" and "vulgarian." His wife, Mary Emma Flood, was never accepted in the social whirl and was often the brunt of ridicule and gossip. Neighbors agreed that Flood, son of poor Irish immigrants, who had grown up in Staten Island slums, lacked the breeding that they considered essential for admission to the coveted ranks of society's inner circle.

Flood came to California during the Gold Rush, dabbling in mining, carriage making and carpentry. Eventually he became proprietor of the Auction Lunch Room, a moderately successful saloon in San Francisco.

During the 1860s, Flood and business partner William O'Brien sold the saloon to become stockbrokers. Few played the market as skillfully. In 1873, in an expanded partnership with James G. Fair and John W. MacKay, they struck the Big Bonanza in the Nevada Comstock. Thereafter, the four men became known as the "Silver Kings." Theirs was the single most valuable silver discovery in the history of the West. Before its exhaustion in 1897, the mine yielded almost $136 million.

Ornate Linden Towers *became the epitome of extravagance and Menlo Park luxury.*

A MOST LEGENDARY MANSION

Of all the great houses in early Menlo Park, none became more legendary than *Linden Towers*, home of James C. Flood. Completed in 1880 on the east side of Middlefield Road, the mansion gave new meaning to the word ostentation. It was the Peninsula's largest and the most lavish. Construction costs were in excess of $1 million.

It was a 43-room mass of turrets, cupolas and gables, capped by a striking 150-foot tower. It was almost seven stories in height. Critics scrutinized the glaring white structure, trimmed in gold with a black slate roof, and termed it a "beautiful atrocity," resembling a wedding cake designed by a "mad confectioner."

Chandeliers were crystal, bronze, and silver. Rooms were panelled in exotic woods. The interior was characterized by rich wall hangings, marble statuary and wood furniture. The dining room table seated 40 and the high-backed chairs were so heavy few could maneuver them without assistance. Bathroom fixtures were fashioned of Comstock silver.

The Towers, as the house was usually known, sat on 600 acres. Flood employed 120 gardeners to keep the grounds presentable. Six cared exclusively for 22 acres of lawn. One full-time worker repaired and painted the white picket fence surrounding the estate. (The mile-long brick wall, still existent along Middlefield Road, was constructed by James L. Flood in 1907.)

The property was sold for the Lindenwood subdivision in 1934. Because of its elegance, much of the interior was acquired by Hollywood movie studios. The structure itself was demolished.

Former President Ulysses S. Grant and wife Julia, along with their son Frederick Dent, visited Menlo Park in 1879.

Cora Jane (Jennie) Flood sat with her "Silver King" father for this portrait.

MENLO PARK BECAME DESTINATION OF ASPIRING POLITICIANS

During the nineteenth century, aspiring national politicians, attracted by the wealth of Menlo Park, came to view a visitation as almost obligatory.

Such at least was the case in September 1879, when former President Ulysses S. Grant, accompanied by his wife Julia and son Frederick Dent (Buck), arrived in San Francisco from Japan after a two-and-a-half year round-the-world tour. Grant had convinced himself that another presidential nomination was within his grasp.

Included in the general's Peninsula itinerary was a multi-course garden luncheon at *Linden Towers*, the yet-to-be completed Menlo Park home of James C. Flood.

While at Menlo Park, handsome young Buck Grant became acquainted with Flood's daughter, the very eligible Cora Jane (Jennie). Romance blossomed. Miss Flood accompanied the Grant party throughout California. At least according to legend, though Jennie was "inclined toward headaches" and spent most of her time with the older ladies, the pair was betrothed.

But after Grant's party finally headed east, there appears to have been no further communication between the pair. Jennie Flood never married. General Grant also failed in his attempt for renomination.

During the 1930s, Beltramo's liquor establishment on El Camino Real was cherished as an important town landmark. Pictured is Mrs. Alexander Beltramo with sons John and Dan.

㊲ BELTRAMO'S, A REVERED INSTITUTION

Giovanni (John) Beltramo, a native of Northern Italy, arrived in California in 1882 to work in the Cupertino vineyards of San Francisco and Menlo Park attorney John T. Doyle.

Eight years later, with his family, Beltramo moved to Menlo Park, establishing a home and retail liquor outlet on Ringwood Avenue between Middlefield and Bay Road. In 1904, he built a complex of buildings at 183 Glenwood Avenue. Beltramo's, including a boarding house frequented by immigrant Italian workers, became a landmark. His was the only retail-wholesale liquor establishment between Redwood City and Mountain View. Menlo Park residents made pilgrimages to Beltramo's to purchase wine and whiskey. Farmers from the surrounding area came in wagons, usually buying adequate amounts to last for a month.

Beltramo's suffered financial setbacks resulting first from the law making it illegal to sell alcohol in the neighborhood of Stanford University and then by federal Prohibition of the 1920s.

Following the repeal of Prohibition laws, Giovanni's son, Alexander, plunged into the business anew. Besides returning to sales, he established The Oasis Beer Garden in an old Camp Fremont building on the west side of County Road north of San Francisquito Creek. This became a haunt of Stanford students acclaimed for its hamburgers.

Still constrained by the law forbidding the sale of alcoholic beverages within 1.5 miles of the university, Beltramo, in 1935, measured off the distance precisely, finding himself in front of a garage in the 1500 block of El Camino Real. He acquired the property and converted it into a bar and retail liquor establishment.

The new Beltramo's became a mecca for residents of Menlo Park, Atherton, and the still-dry Palo Alto. The 1.5-mile dry zone around the university was lifted in 1979.

Giovanni Beltramo (1882)

The couple married in 1887. The always unhappy marriage ended with his death a decade later.

Gertrude Atherton

George B. Atherton

㊳CALIFORNIA'S MOST FAMED WOMAN AUTHOR

Gertrude Franklin Horn (1857-1948), born on San Francisco's Rincon Hill during the Gold Rush, eloped with handsome George B. Atherton, son of the well-known merchant, in 1877. They made their home with his parents at *Valparaiso Park*.

She found life in Menlo Park filled with boring hours of genteel conversation, apparently endless dinners, and fatiguing visits from neighbors. Much to the disgust of a disapproving mother-in-law, Gertrude longed to become a writer.

Fortuitously, at least for Gertrude, husband George, an alcoholic, died in 1887. The widow headed for the East to follow her dreams. Ironically, later while in Europe, she came to recognize a fascination people had for colorful, unexplored romance of Old California in the era "before the gringo came."

Over time she achieved recognition as California's leading woman author. Her style, reflecting her personality, was somewhat cynical but vigorous. She gently mocked Victorian customs and attitudes. Her heroines were amazingly strong, human, and sometimes sexual. Critics said she wielded her pen with the same skill as a surgeon wields a scalpel. "The moment I take my pen in my hand the ink turns to gall," she wrote early in her career.

This literary matron published dozens of novels, histories, collections of essays, and short stories. There were almost sixty books. Additionally she wrote millions of words for magazines and newspapers. No other California writer was as versatile or prolific, but her popularity was greater in Europe than in California, and today she commands only minimal respect as a writer.

Dominga de Goñi Atherton, Gertrude's mother-in-law, prided herself on her conservative Spanish-Catholic dignity. She never approved of Gertrude's chosen profession.

A CONTROVERSIAL WOMAN

Tranquil Menlo Park wasn't Gertrude Atherton's cup of tea. "I often wondered if life anywhere else in the whole wide world were as dull...the time came when I could stand Menlo Park no longer."

The lady was unquestionably an intellectual, a trait which the ultra-conservative Atherton family believed was distinctly unfeminine. She felt hopelessly isolated. Once it was suggested that she write a novel about Menlo Park. Gertrude responded that such a project would cause her to "fall over asleep from sheer boredom."

Nevertheless, the idea of writing appealed to her. Her first known try at fiction, in 1883, was titled *The Randolphs of Redwood*. This is a sizzling expose, thinly disguised, of one family in the drunken and notoriously scandalous high society then inhabiting the Peninsula.

Atherton sold this work to *The Argonaut*, a locally published periodical. The sordid tales created a sensation and a general brouhaha in which she delighted. Though published pseudonymously, in an effort to protect the family name, her identity leaked. She received the social cold shoulder. The Atherton family was mortified.

Throughout her adult life, controversy swirled around this woman author.

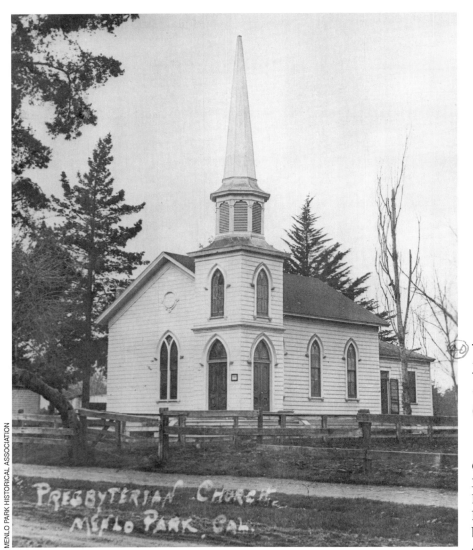

Protestants formed Menlo Park Presbyterian Church in 1872.

MENLO PARK PRESBYTERIAN CHURCH

Menlo Park Presbyterian Church, organized November 30, 1873, was the town's first Protestant house of worship. Funds for construction of a building were gathered from contributions offered by Milton S. Latham, Thomas H. Selby, Faxon D. Atherton, Charles N. Felton and Judge Henry P. Coon. Though Presbyterian by doctrine, in that it was the single Protestant church of the area, the early congregation was comprised of many denominations.

A large site for a building, at 700 Santa Cruz Avenue, was deeded to the church by Thomas H. Selby for the sum of $1. Thereon, during the summer of 1874, at a cost of $4,000, a white, steepled New England-style church with a Gothic facade was erected. The sanctuary seated 168.

Sunday morning education for children was offered under the superintendency of Judge Coon. From the start, 35 students were in regular attendance. The first minister, who lived with his family in the back room of the church, was Rev. H.P. Harron.

The church was supported by pew rent and offerings. An 1890 document indicates that a double pew, depending upon its location, could be rented for between $10 and $50 a year. Rent for single pews was $2 to $10. Financially, the early church fared well, thanks largely to the generous donations of Leland and Jane Stanford.

San Francisco Judge Henry P. Coon provided the impetus behind creation of the new church.

HENRY P. COON

In 1873, one of San Francisco's leading citizens, the versatile Judge Henry P. Coon (1822-1884) acquired a 300-acre estate, *Adelante Villa*, as a summer place south of San Francisquito Creek.

Coon became the guiding force behind the establishment of Menlo Park Presbyterian Church. Over the years, pastors came and went, but during the early years, the faithful Coon was always there. When one of the church's regular ministers failed to appear, the ever-ready Coon took to the pulpit. He was admired for eloquent sermons.

He was a Gold Rush arrival to California in 1853 and opened a medical practice. Indeed, by training and profession, Coon was a medical doctor. Additionally, he was a lawyer, druggist and police judge. He was two-term mayor of San Francisco.

Coon opposed lenient handling of criminals and played a significant role in the vigilante uprising in San Francisco in 1856. He was the grandfather of San Mateo County Superior Court Judge Maxwell McNutt.

By the 1880s, *Adelante Villa* was dilapidated and overgrown with trees and weeds. The property was sold to Leland Stanford for use to accommodate members of the university faculty.

Maxwell McNutt, grandson of Henry Coon, grew up in Menlo Park. During the 1930s, voters elected him to be judge of the superior court.

Leland and Jane Stanford sat for a photograph with their son in Paris shortly before the boy's premature death.

STANFORDS PREFER THE TOWN OF MENLO PARK

When the Stanfords arrived on the Peninsula, Palo Alto was a yellow wheat field and Menlo Park a quiet hamlet. The only excitement was the arrival and departure of trains. Still, for years, Leland and Jane Stanford preferred Menlo Park to the virtually non-existent Palo Alto. Initially, when they considered construction of a university, their hope had been to locate the institution in Menlo Park. Only when difficulties arose regarding land title did they opt to build in Santa Clara County.

Nevertheless, the couple always looked favorably upon Menlo Park and commonly used the depot. They also went to great expense to make the hamlet a better place to live. When Stanford died in June 1893, his remains were brought to Menlo Park for removal to the Stanford mausoleum. The depot was draped in black crepe. Thereafter, Jane Lathrop Stanford ceased using Menlo Park depot.

Mrs. Stanford lived until 1905. Upon her death, in accordance with her wishes, her body, accompanied by university president David Starr Jordan, was returned from Honolulu, where death had occurred, and taken by train to Menlo Park. But she is interred at the university.

Jane Stanford assumed leadership of the kindergarten movement in America. She established the Free Kindergarten in Menlo Park (1885).

JANE STANFORD'S CONTRIBUTIONS TO THE TOWN

The year was 1885 when Jane Stanford apparently first became aware of the many "little urchins tumbling in the Menlo dust."

For some time, she had been part of the kindergarten movement in the United States. During the early 1870s, there had been fewer than 40 kindergartens in the nation. By 1887, there were 40 such in the San Francisco Bay Area alone. Mrs. Stanford supported eight of them. Menlo Park's waifs gave impetus to a Stanford-supported kindergarten for the town. It wasn't long before it had been created in a small, well-equipped house with a grassy lawn on which the children played.

By the end of 1885, between 35 and 40 students were in regular attendance. Youngsters, ranging in age from three to seven, were trained with dumbbells and learned to march. Mrs. Stanford was allegedly much relieved to know that the little ones were off the street.

Jane Stanford was appalled by a universal lack of acceptable singing voices at the Presbyterian Church and called for the formation of a choir. In 1884, she hired Professor J.H. Elwood of the San Jose State Normal School to visit the town once per week to teach music and, in the process, improve the quality of music at the church.

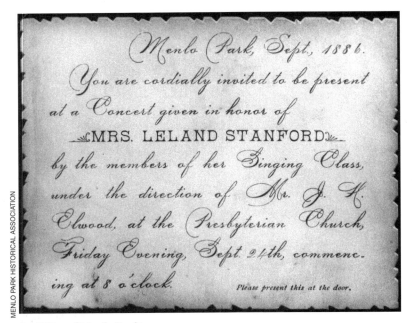

Inability of Menlo Park's Protestants to sing on key, prompted Mrs. Stanford to establish a voice class. Attendance became a social highlight of the town.

Jane Lathrop Stanford

THE STANFORDS AND THE PRESBYTERIANS

Although the Stanfords were avowed Episcopalians, the Presbyterian Church was the town's only Protestant house of worship. Thus, Mrs. Stanford went to have a look at it. Rain was falling and she found the minister busily shuffling pans in the effort to catch water dripping though the leaky roof.

This photograph shows the interior of the original Presbyterian Church.

At Stanford expense, the church acquired a new roof. The building was repaired and painted inside and out. The center aisle was newly carpeted and the antique melodeon was replaced by a small organ. In 1885, Jane Stanford ordered construction of a substantial dwelling near the corner of County Road and Ravenswood Avenue as the parsonage for the church.

When in residence, the Stanfords attended Presbyterian services. Their attendance brought the wealthy of the area flocking to the church and it prospered.

When an Episcopal congregation was formed in 1886, the Stanfords shifted their allegiance to the new church.

Thurlow Lodge's *new owner renamed the grand house* **Sherwood Hall.** *This is a front view from the lawn.*

THURLOW LODGE BECOMES SHERWOOD HALL

Mary Frances Sherwood Hopkins, widow of transcontinental railroad builder Mark Hopkins, was one of the wealthiest women in the world, with an estimated worth at $70 million.

Shortly after the death of her husband in the 1880s, the childless Mrs. Hopkins had adopted 21-year old Timothy Nolan (1859-1936), who had grown up in the Hopkins home.

She set him up as treasurer of Southern Pacific with an annual salary of $10,000. In 1882, Timothy married his mother's favorite niece, receiving then a gift of $100,000 and an apartment in San Francisco. Not long thereafter, as a Christmas present in 1888, the couple was presented a massive estate in Menlo Park. This was the former Barron-Latham property. Timothy called his spread *Sherwood Hall.*

The couple divided time between San Francisco and Menlo Park. Timothy wanted to make the Menlo estate self-supporting. He established Sherwood Hall Nursery, advertising himself as a grower of trees, plants and shrubs and sold seeds. With offices in San Francisco, the company employed 60 Chinese laborers in Menlo Park. In 1893, the name of the nursery was changed to the Sunset Seed and Plant Company. During the 1890s, Hopkins raised 250 varieties of chrysanthemums and cultivated 10,000 plots of roses. Eventually there were 25 huge glasshouses on the estate.

Mary (May) Hopkins

Timothy Hopkins

Edgar Mills

Darius Ogden Mills

While D.O. Mills returned to New York, Edgar remained behind to manage the family's vast estates in the West.

CALIFORNIA HISTORICAL SOCIETY. FN-31945

STABLE AND DEPENDABLE EDGAR MILLS

Born into a well-to-do Westchester County, New York family, Edgar Mills (1827-1893) was trained as a civil engineer. While still young, he was employed in New York making surveys for the Hudson River Railroad.

But, infected by rumors of gold in California, even before official announcement of the discovery, he began the 12,000-mile sea voyage to San Francisco. His elder brother, Darius Ogden Mills, followed him West. D.O. Mills was almost immediately successful, establishing himself in Sacramento as a banker and a decade later moving to San Francisco where, with William C. Ralston in 1864, he became president of the Bank of California. He also invested in the Nevada Comstock and in the construction of railroads throughout the West.

After the elder brother's move to San Francisco, Edgar Mills became a banker, purchasing D.O. Mills' earlier bank holdings. And, especially after the creation of the Bank of California, the stable and dependable Edgar acted as the brother's agent in Sacramento and the Mother Lode.

D.O. Mills returned to New York in 1880. Meanwhile, Edgar remained in the West looking after family investments. As such, he served as president of the Eureka & Palisade, the powerful Virginia & Truckee and the Carson and Colorado railroads.

Edgar Mills was comfortable living in opulent style at 1950 California Street. After many prominent neighbors acquired property at Menlo Park, Mills purchased a summer home there as well.

The still-surviving Mills home has seen service for numerous endeavors.

47 MENLO PROPERTY OF EDGAR MILLS

Edgar Mills purchased the Menlo Park house in September 1880. The original 21-room Italianate structure had been built on present-day Noel Drive between 1868 and 1870 for T. Lemmon Meyer, a director of the Menlo Park & Santa Cruz Turnpike Road Company. In 1875, Meyer sold it to Alexander Gansl, who renovated the house, planted extensive gardens, and laid out pathways.

During the five years of Gansl's ownership, the place became a popular gambling house. Wealthy San Francisco businessmen arrived for weekend stays. Stakes were high. It was said that $50,000 could be won or lost there in a single evening.

Upon acquisition, Mills renovated the structure and it was substantially enlarged. The spacious living room with inlaid walnut woodwork was celebrated for its 16-foot ceiling and luxurious Victorian furnishings. In 1887, while maintaining the house and a small amount of property immediately around it, Mills subdivided the substantial grounds into 100 home lots.

Sometime after Mills' death, the house sold to Emma Noel, who rented it out as a summer residence. During World War I, she lent the house to the Army for use as the Camp Fremont Officers Club. At that time, for Army entertainments, the carriage house facing Laurel Street was converted into a ballroom.

For a brief period after the war, the house became the Laurel Court Hotel. That is until 1926 when Miss Noel leased it to Major Royal W. Park. He opened it as the Pacific Coast Military Academy, an exclusive private institution for boys from five to fourteen years of age.

Helen Wildman purchased the house for $65,000 in 1946. She converted it into a restaurant known for years as the Marie Antoinette Inn. It then housed the Bright Eagle antique shop, and it is presently used for office suites.

Long the village graveyard, Holy Cross Cemetery was acquired by the Church of the Nativity and consecrated as a Roman Catholic burial ground in 1883.

48 HOLY CROSS CEMETERY

November 18, 1883. Well west of town, along Santa Cruz Avenue, five crosses, one which rose to a height of 14 feet, were erected in the town's longtime graveyard.

Initially 10 acres, these grounds having passed to the control of the Church of the Nativity, Roman Catholic Bishop Patrick William Riordan moved about the property sprinkling holy water. In the process, he named and consecrated Holy Cross Cemetery.

Still active in the last years of the twentieth century, at which time there had been almost 5,000 burials, Holy Cross is one of Menlo Park's most historic shrines. The oldest surviving marker dates from 1866. Nevertheless, there is some evidence that the burial ground may have been used as the town's graveyard as early as the 1850s.

Many graves are still marked by simple wood crosses. Among the larger plots is one for the family of famed attorney John T. Doyle (1819-1906). Other names of note are Alejandra Atherton Rathbone (1844-1913), Atherton Macondray (1871-1920) and Elena Atherton Selby (1901-1918).

During the early 1950s, Stanford University officials ordered relocation of all remains from the St. Denis burial ground on the hill. These were transferred to Holy Cross Cemetery in 1953 for interment in a common grave. A monument near the Santa Cruz Avenue entrance to the cemetery marks this location.

IRISH HORTICULTURAL WIZARD BRINGS FAME TO TOWN

By the 1870s, Menlo Park was already acclaimed as one of Northern California's most magnificent beauty spots. And one of the men most responsible for this reputation was Irish-born Michael Lynch (1847-1905). A graduate of the Royal Botanical Gardens of Dublin with advanced study in Liverpool and London, Lynch arrived in California in 1869. His first employment was as superintendent of the grounds at the home of Faxon Atherton's son-in-law Major Lawrence Rathbone.

After a brief respite working in Contra Costa County, Lynch returned to the Peninsula in 1880 at the behest of James C. Flood, who retained him to care for the Rudolf Ulrich-designed formal gardens at *Linden Towers*. This amazing burst of color was defined by vine-covered walls highlighted with gaslights, circular flower beds and a huge multi-tiered fountain.

Flood died in 1889 and Lynch was enticed by Timothy Hopkins to assume the same responsibilities at *Sherwood Hall*.

Lynch retired from the service of others in 1892 to establish his own Menlo Park Nursery along Oak Grove Avenue. In addition to open air gardens with acres of flower beds, he constructed 15 greenhouses. Lynch used his own stock exclusively in landscaping Menlo Park's Holy Cross Cemetery, St. Patrick's Seminary, and the Grass Valley (Empire Mine) home of William Bourn. Additionally he assisted in the landscaping of the Stanford campus.

Michael Lynch, standing, as superintendent of Sherwood Hall, *planted the largest violet field in the nation. During the twentieth century, the City of Menlo Park adopted the purple posy as the town's official flower.*

Plants propagated at Lynch's nursery along Oak Grove Avenue highlighted important landscape designs throughout California.

Maria O'Brien Coleman commissioned this elegant house, completed in 1882. Towers tumbled in the earthquake of 1906.

⑤⓪ A SURVIVING VICTORIAN

Immense amounts of lumber were shipped to Menlo Park in 1880, earmarked for construction of the balconied Victorian country estate being built for Maria O'Brien Coleman, the sister of silver king William O'Brien.

This home was designed by prominent English-born architect Augustus Laver (1834-1898), who had already achieved local fame with his design for James C. Flood's *Linden Towers*.

Two years in the building, the great Italianate gingerbread structure reportedly cost $100,000. This 22-room, double-walled house, completed in 1882, was notable for the richness of its architectural detail.

There were polished hardwood floors throughout. A broad staircase led to the second floor. There were marble sink tops and crystal chandeliers. A roof, above a curved veranda, was supported by Corinthian columns. First floor windows were highlighted by flanking pilasters. Second floor windows were arched.

The structure withstood the 1906 earthquake without damage. On the other hand, nearby St. Patrick's Seminary had to close because of extensive damage. Agreement was reached to use the Coleman mansion as a home for seminarians during reconstruction of St. Patrick's. They occupied the residence until 1909.

BILL WARTO

In 1925, the one-time
Coleman home became
Peninsula School.
The structure is still
in use today.

⑤ GHOSTLY TALES FROM INSIDE GREAT HOUSE

Maria O'Brien Coleman inherited $4 million from her brother, silver king William O'Brien, when he died in 1878. Shortly thereafter, she acquired 165 Menlo Park acres and began construction of a Victorian home, which she envisioned would be a wedding gift for her son.

Mrs. Coleman's son, James Valentine Coleman (1852-1919), was married to the comely Carmelita Parrott Nuthall (1861-1885) in 1880. He, a handsome 28-year old, held a seat in the state assembly. She, 19, was the granddaughter of San Francisco banker John Parrott.

Coleman returned to the couple's San Francisco home on Taylor Street at 5 a.m. July 8, 1885. The wife jumped from her bed to unpack his valise. A loaded revolver fell to the floor. It discharged, the bullet ripping into Carmelita, fracturing a rib and exiting her back. Police investigated, albeit gently, given the station of the dead woman's husband. They deemed the death "accidental."

Assemblyman Coleman "lost interest" in the Peninsula house (completed three years before and not occupied) and never lived there. The palatial Victorian stood vacant for years.

Peninsula School acquired it in 1925. Not long thereafter, Carmelita, or at least her spirit, was supposed to have made an appearance. Strange stories circulated. Children noticed shimmering lights and heard footsteps stalking in the deserted upper floors. Spooked pets refused to enter the building. For years, there have been reports of sightings of a beautiful young woman in a diaphanous green dress. School spokesmen claimed that Carmelita's "ghost" added color and charisma to the house.

PENINSULA SCHOOL ARCHIVE

*Carmelita Parrott
Nuthall Coleman*

PENINSULA SCHOOL ARCHIVE

James Valentine Coleman

For years, Duff & Doyle's general store was a hub of village activity.

52 DUFF & DOYLE'S GENERAL STORE

The town's most famed merchandise emporium opened in April 1874. Established by Murtha Joseph Doyle (1842-1881), it was located at Santa Cruz Avenue and the County Road (El Camino Real). Becoming ill in the late 1870s, Murtha turned the business over to his brother James R. Doyle.

Before doing so, Murtha had decided it would be good business to have a post office in the store and contrived to have himself appointed postmaster (1876). The post office continued to be in the store until 1889, when it was moved to the pharmacy next door.

Business boomed. James Doyle, seeing a need for a partner, concluded an agreement with Michael Duff. Duff & Doyle's became a focal point of the town. This was a general merchandise emporium in the truest sense. Customers found everything from ladies' hats, trousers and off-the-shelf shoes, to tobacco, thread and ribbon, patent medicines, even pickled herring. There were barrels of pickles and crackers. Coffee beans were scooped from 100-pound sacks. Duff & Doyle's carried all forms of farm paraphernalia, including food for stock, blasting powder, and kerosene. They commonly accepted butter, eggs, and chickens in exchange for merchandise.

Remembering his childhood, resident Frank Brady remarked in 1988 that Duff & Doyle's was an old-fashioned country store "such as Norman Rockwell would have been delighted to paint." The business was liquidated during the early 1920s and the brick building razed in 1942.

The determination to have an Episcopal Church in Menlo Park elevated Edward and Mary Tutt Eyre to leadership in the cause to build the Parish of the Holy Trinity.

⑤③ EPISCOPAL PARISH OF THE HOLY TRINITY

The nineteenth-century Gothic-styled church, constructed of rough boards cut from a nearby redwood forest, opened in 1886 as the Episcopal Parish of the Holy Trinity. It quickly became the Peninsula's most politically potent church.

Upon moving to the community in 1876, Menlo Park residents Edward and Mary Tutt Eyre were dismayed that the town possessed no Episcopal Church. The nearest was in Redwood City. A round trip by carriage along rutted roads took five hours. Building an Episcopal church became the Eyres' goal. Land was donated by Edward W. Hopkins, owner of *Vallombrosa*. Enticed by a salary of $50 a month, Redwood City minister William Stowe agreed to come to Menlo Park.

Although the true power behind its establishment was Mary Tutt Eyre, her husband Edward received credit as the organizer. He served as senior warden and sat on the governing board until his death in 1899.

Assisting him on the vestry were Leland Stanford and William James Adams. Adding political clout to the board was Charles N. Felton. Rounding out the vestry's list of notables were Percy Selby and prosperous dry goods merchant George Loomis. No religious institution in the West had ever possessed a governing board as socially and politically prominent.

The structure has been remodeled and moved several times. Presently it is the Church of the Nativity of the Holy Virgin, a Russian Orthodox institution at 1220 Crane Street.

Holy Trinity's choir posed for a photo on the church steps in 1888.

ELOISE LANCESTREMERRE

*Contractor John MacBain
constructed Oak Grove
Villa Hotel in 1887.*

54 OAK GROVE VILLA HOTEL

The contract for construction of the three-story Oak Grove Hotel was awarded to Menlo Park builder John MacBain in 1887. This ornate structure, at Oak Grove Avenue and Merrill Street, became one of the showplaces of the town.

Its structure remained a landmark until the 1960s. Longtime neighbor Eloise Lancestremere remembers that during Prohibition it was one of the area's most celebrated "speakeasies." In later years, it ceased to function as a hotel and was converted into a boarding house.

During the twentieth century, firemen nervously eyed the antique structure. It was declared a firetrap and padlocked. Young firefighters were given the task of developing contingency plans to deal with extinguishing a blaze in such a structure.

One-time Menlo Park Fire Chief George Carter recalls that a blaze of unknown origin broke out in the building on September 4, 1965. Fire quickly swept through the building, leaping to the attic and roof. The chief called in five alarms. Hundreds gathered to witness the last minutes of this landmark.

BEGINNINGS OF STANFORD UNIVERSITY

Dedication of Leland Stanford Junior Memorial University occurred in 1891, four years after laying of a cornerstone.

"The children of California will now be our children," declared a grief-stricken Leland Stanford soon after the death of his 15-year old son in May 1884. The memorial to this beloved boy was to be Leland Stanford Junior Memorial University.

Journalists scoffed that California had as much need for a second university as Switzerland had "for an asylum for decayed sea captains." Critics were incredulous, predicting for years that professors would lecture to half-empty halls. The governor intended to build this new institution on dusty wheat fields of the south Peninsula, a location without town or railroad station. Still, Leland and wife Jane Stanford were undeterred. They devoted their fortune to the task and the university became the most richly endowed educational institution in the world. A cornerstone was laid May 14, 1887. Architecture combined Romanesque and Mission Revival to perpetuate the memory of California's pioneer Spanish settlers. The co-educational university was dedicated October 1, 1891, and opened with a total of 559 students.

"Starkly elegant" is the way some critics described the completed university set among the wheat fields. The Stanford Memorial Arch, pictured, crumbled in the earthquake of 1906.

From its inception, Menlo Park was closely associated with the university, providing the train depot, post and telegraph offices. Most Stanford faculty members, along with university president David Starr Jordan, lived in the town and made the trek to the campus on foot. Empty houses in town were quickly rented.

By the 1890s, the town was celebrated for its many residences, not only great mansions but ordinary homes as well. Pictured is the William A. Doyle residence.

ELOISE LANGESTREMERE

MENLO PARK HISTORICAL ASSOCIATION

This photo of the Wells, Fargo & Co. Express office seems to contradict the booming nature of town business during the 1890s.

AN IMPORTANT TURNING POINT

Few turning points are as easily definable as the year 1891 was in the saga of Menlo Park. Nearby, an army of workers was putting final touches on the university. New homes were being constructed and vacant cottages refurbished to house the faculty and staff. The town, with a population of 400 the previous year, was rapidly becoming a political center; California's two U.S. Senators, Stanford and Felton, were neighbors.

Responding to the town's new status, Menlo Park Hotel proprietor Martin Kuck undertook a complete renovation to assure that his was an attractive place of rustication for its many summer visitors. Most locals agreed that Kuck's was the town's only decent place to lunch.

Once insignificant Duff & Doyle's general store on Santa Cruz Avenue now carried the largest stock of merchandise in San Mateo County. Four full-time clerks catered to a constant stream of customers. Town businesses boomed. In October, a bicycle rental shop opened adjacent to the barbershop. Bikes rented for 25 cents an hour.

During the last week of September, the town became crowded with hundreds of students and professors with towering piles of trunks. Trains brought distinguished guests to Menlo Park for the October 1st dedication of the university. There were 5,000 in attendance.

Few California towns since the Gold Rush experienced such a rapid awakening.

Cedro Cottage, *set on 24 acres, was purchased by the Stanfords in 1882. This "Victorian jewel box of a house" became a special sanctuary for Jane Stanford and her son. Ariel Lathrop, one of Mrs. Stanford's four brothers, lived there for a time.*

57 CEDRO COTTAGE

Ariel Lathrop

Town residents came to know *Cedro Cottage* from the white picket fence which surrounded it. In the immediate years after the Stanfords arrived on the Peninsula, the cottage was occupied by Jane Stanford's brother Ariel Lathrop and became a popular hideaway for Mrs. Stanford and son Leland Jr. At different times, various superintendents of the Stanford Stock Farm, including the famed trainer Charles Marvin, also lived there later.

With the opening of the university in 1891, the cottage took on a new existence. Accommodations for professors were at a premium. Undoubtedly because he was the father of three, Oliver Peebles Jenkins, professor of physiology and histology, was offered *Cedro Cottage*.

Mrs. Jenkins was ecstatic. "We quickly jumped out of the carriage...and began to explore the surroundings. The children were wild with joy. Here were seven acres of land covered with trees, shrubbery, vines, roses, walks, drives, orchards, stables, a big barn where we found the Chinaman whose duty it had been to keep the place in order....Can you imagine our gladness? We obtained the key and went into the house, where we found beautifully furnished rooms."

In fact, the gingerbread cottage had two large bedrooms adjoined by a full bathroom with chain-flushing toilet, washbasin and large galvanized bathtub. It had been fully piped for hot and cold water, although there was neither telephone nor electricity. There was a pantry and fine garden along with detached servants quarters. Rent was $30 a month.

Goodall transformed Petite Forêt *into a garden paradise.*

MARINER CREATES IDYLLIC EXISTENCE

Few country homes conveyed a sweeter sense of rest and contentment than *Petite Forêt*, the Glenwood Avenue estate of Captain Charles Goodall (1824-1899). Born in Somersetshire, England, Goodall came to California during the Gold Rush. He was politically astute and served both as a California Assemblyman and as Harbor Master for the Port of San Francisco.

This well-respected mariner was the senior member of the shipping firm of Goodall, Perkins & Company, whose ships sailed the Pacific from Mexican ports to Puget Sound. Besides other duties, Goodall served as president of the Pacific Coast Steamship Company, the Pacific Coast Whaling Company and as vice president of the Oceanic Steamship Company. He was also a confidant of Leland Stanford and a trustee of the university.

At *Petite Forêt*, Goodall created a garden wonderland characterized by beds of annuals with shrubbery and flora of the daintiest form. He maintained a herd of deer. Flocks of black Australian swans sailed majestically and noiselessly in his fountains. There were aquariums of goldfish. A band of Shetland ponies gamboled about the estate.

After his death, *Petite Forêt* sold to Charles M. Hays, president of Southern Pacific Railroad. Thereafter, it was acquired by photographer Albert Hahn.

Captain Charles Goodall

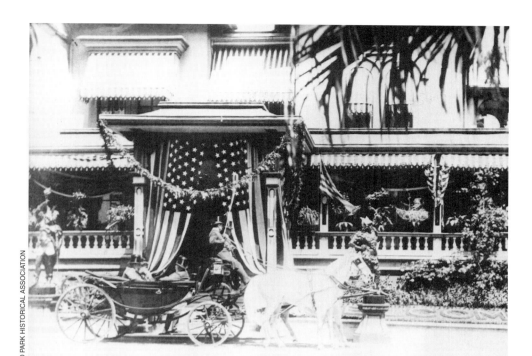

President Harrison was served lunch by the Stanfords at Palo Alto.

59 PRESIDENTIAL VISIT, 1891

President Benjamin Harrison was aloof and distant. He lacked warmth and was far from being the nation's best loved chief executive. Nevertheless, presidential visits to California were rare. Thus, for a week in May 1891, his comings and goings dominated the thinking of Westerners.

That the president would spend a weekend at the exclusive Del Monte Hotel in Monterey surprised no one. But that he would detrain at sleepy Menlo Park was cause for excitement. There were displays of roses and hundreds of people crowded the depot platform when the train stopped. Children of the town's kindergarten, wearing paper hats and dressed in white, were drawn up in two straight lines. They broke mechanically into song as the president stoically inspected their ranks. Townsfolk cheered, although most were offended that Harrison mumbled not a single kind word to the youngsters.

Seldom had residents seen such a gorgeous assembly of vehicles. Virtually all the town dignitaries took part in the reception. Luminaries donned linen dusters for the carriage parade to inspect the recently completed university. Stanford himself did the tour. Harrison's reaction to the new institution was disappointing.

At *Palo Alto*, Mrs. Stanford supervised the spreading of an elegant epicurean repast, a sit-down luncheon for 40. Thereafter, Harrison and his wife participated in the planting of two redwood trees. Harrison made a courtesy call at *Felton Gables* and stopped at *Sherwood Hall* for a glass of wine with Timothy Hopkins before entraining for Del Monte. Almost audible sighs of relief could be heard throughout the town.

Benjamin Harrison

Central Grammar School opened in 1893 and burned in 1912.

60 CENTRAL GRAMMAR SCHOOL

The town's first public schoolhouse, built at a cost of $2,000 and located near Crane Street on Oak Grove Avenue, opened in October 1874. In Victorian style, there were separate entries and segregated playgrounds for boys and girls.

That small school lasted until June 1893 when a new two-story Central Grammar School opened on the east side of County Road south of Glenwood. The event was marked with a grand Saturday night reception. A throng surged through the building, admiring each of the four classrooms and the modern workmanship before gathering in the Assembly Hall to hear a piano concert. The classic school structure was erected by Menlo Park contractor John MacBain. There was an armory room and a library on the second floor along with a completely finished basement used for recreation during the rainy season.

School traditionally recessed for six weeks beginning in April. The vacation was set to coincide with apricot picking season, when "every boy and girl should join in assisting the fruit-growers, and save them the necessity of employing Chinese."

On October 2, 1912, while painters were scraping peeling paint from the building, fire was discovered in the belfry and, despite the gallant efforts of firefighters, it was consumed by flames and destroyed. A new Central Grammar School was erected in 1914 and in constant use until declared unsafe in 1963.

The Chinese laundry as it appeared before destruction in 1954. Chinese buildings and homes were usually kept shuttered because of the town's children's practice of showering them with bricks and stones, "Irish confetti," as it was called.

MENLO PARK HISTORICAL ASSOCIATION

CHINATOWN

By the early years of the twentieth century, Menlo Park possessed the largest Chinatown on the Peninsula. The precise size of the Chinese population was unknown. There may have been as many as 50. Additionally, scores of Chinese cooks and servants were employed by owners of surrounding estates and at Stanford University.

In Chinatown, along both sides of Glenwood Avenue between San Antonio and the railroad tracks, there were several laundries, a boarding house, a gambling house, and a number of homes, usually described as "shacks." Chinese males frequently sat along the road smoking "peculiar long pipes with small brass bowls." Caucasian residents believed this was opium.

Ursula Leonardi, whose Italian mother had the unique experience of working in a Chinese laundry, recalls that the population was largely male. Men traditionally dressed in Chinese costume with round, black silk caps. All men wore queues.

The two-story Wo Sing Laundry had a school on the second floor which Chinese youngsters attended in the afternoons to receive instruction in their parents' language.

Though still a young girl when she saw it, Eloise Lancestremere (b. 1908) clearly remembers the gambling house into which she was once sent with a message. In the huge room were many white-clothed card tables. Lights hanging from the ceiling illuminated each table. Around the edge of the room were bunks on which Chinese reclined.

Lancestremere notes that from 1915-1920 university students gravitated to the gambling house on weekends. Many Chinese from San Francisco, especially at night, also came to gamble. These were high stakes games; noisy fights were common. For recreation on weekends, many local Chinese went to San Francisco, returning on the "theater train" late at night.

Menlo Park Chinese were neither liked nor well treated by Caucasian residents. Kids commonly threw rocks and bricks at their homes, probably accounting for the fact that Chinese houses were almost always tightly shuttered.

MENLO PARK HISTORICAL ASSOCIATION

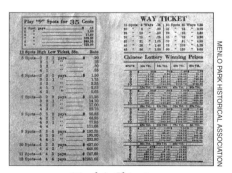

MENLO PARK HISTORICAL ASSOCIATION

Menlo's Chinatown was celebrated for its many games of chance.

MacBain built or modified scores of town buildings. Frank Roach's blacksmith shop was among them.

John MacBain, the town's leading politician, also was Menlo Park's principal builder.

MASTER BUILDER AND POLITICAL GIANT

When he died, political colleagues heaped accolades on John MacBain (1849-1927). The longtime Menlo Park resident had served four terms on the County Board of Supervisors. Upon his first election in 1904, there wasn't a foot of paved road in the south county. MacBain's dream was to give constituents a system of perfect roads. By 1927, as a result of his efforts, Middlefield Road and the State Highway (El Camino Real), Atherton, Fair Oaks and Oak Grove avenues had been macadamized.

A carpenter by training, the Nova Scotia-born MacBain was enticed to the Peninsula in 1878 to participate in construction of James Flood's *Linden Towers*. Thereafter, he launched into business for himself. Although listed in the city directory simply as "Carpenter and Builder," he rapidly acquired status as the town's leading contractor.

During the 1880s and 1890s, he undertook scores of projects. He built Pioneer Hall on the east side of County Road north of Oak Grove. The hall opened with a grand ball in 1886. It housed a barbershop and was used as the site of Friday night dance lessons. He erected a boarding house and the Oak Grove Villa Hotel, serving there briefly as proprietor. When booming business made extra shelving necessary at Duff & Doyle's general store, it was installed by MacBain. He added onto Frank Roach's blacksmith shop and the town's original schoolhouse.

He was a member of Menlo Park Presbyterian and built the church's first manse on Santa Cruz Avenue.

The original Sequoia High School building in Redwood City was erected by MacBain. Until after World War II, high school students from Menlo Park were bussed there.

⑥³ SKILLS ACCLAIMED IN TOWN AND BEYOND

Many of Menlo Park's better known structures were built or modified by MacBain. After the death of Faxon Atherton, MacBain transformed *Valparaiso Park* into an exclusive boys' school for educator Ira D. Hoitt. A luxurious $12,000 stable at Timothy Hopkins' *Sherwood Hall* was built by him. When San Francisco banker Herbert Fleishhacker purchased *Glen-Eyre* in 1910, remodeling and renovation were undertaken by MacBain.

His skill was also appreciated beyond the town. He was general contractor for an eight-story office building in San Francisco and builder of the American Theater. During construction of Stanford University, MacBain was retained to build a number of structures, notably the steam laundry and the gymnasium. In Redwood City, he undertook a $500,000 project erecting Sequoia, the county's first high school building.

Home construction came to be his specialty. Among his favorites were the Samuel Knight house in Hillsborough and the Edward W. Hopkins home in Menlo Park. He worked on the homes of Leland Stanford and wheat mogul Frederick McNear.

MacBain had difficulty with the concept of "vacation." When asked near the end of his career, he reported having taken only one in 50 years.

John MacBain posed in formal garb for his campaign literature when he ran for the San Mateo County Board of Supervisors.

Convent of the Sacred Heart as it appeared when it opened. Still-existent, the structure is little changed.

64 # CONVENT OF THE SACRED HEART

Located along Valparaiso Avenue, a few hundred yards west of present-day Menlo School and College, is Sacred Heart Academy.

Its most impressive feature is the austere three-story convent designed by San Francisco architect Charles Devlin. Digging for the foundation began in 1897. Once, this ominous-looking building served as the convent for the teaching Mesdames of the Sacred Heart, and as both classrooms and student dormitories.

Between 1898 and 1984, the institution was a bastion of orthodox Catholicism taught by strict, semi-cloistered French nuns. Graduation lists include names of leading Peninsula families. Young girls were schooled and disciplined. Talking wasn't allowed between classes. Girls curtseyed to the nuns and silently walked corridors at least an arm's length from any other student. Only French was spoken at meals. Girls were seldom allowed to leave campus. Most thought little of the food, especially the Sunday fare, traditionally rabbit stew, which the nuns insisted was chicken. Punishment was by public humiliation.

Uniformed girls of the Convent of the Sacred Heart, photographed in 1912.

Until the 1950s, the institution was virtually self-sufficient. School authorities cultivated vegetables and raised their own cows. The old barn, a landmark of the property, was finally dismantled in 1990. The building suffered major earthquake damage in 1906 when bricks fell, a sandstone arcade crumbled and the roof collapsed. In that the temblor occurred during Easter vacation, there was no loss of life; few girls were in the building at the time. Rubble, still visible around the building, was simply pushed into the courtyard.

There was almost no damage in the earthquake of 1989. However, fearing another quake, officials closed the building. Parts reopened in summer 1997 at a cost of $5 million for retrofitting and renovation. Presently known as Sacred Heart Schools, the institution became co-educational in 1984.

St. Patrick's Seminary, east of Middlefield Road, opened in 1898.

ST. PATRICK'S SEMINARY

Some refer to graduates of St. Patrick's Seminary, as "the Menlo Park brotherhood."

For decades after it opened in 1898, it was the only Roman Catholic seminary on the Pacific slope. Run by the Society of Sulpice, an order of secular priests organized in France (1641) and dedicated to the formation of a diocesan clergy, the seminary provided priests to the entire Province of the Pacific — California, Oregon, Washington and British Columbia.

The Charles Devlin-designed, red brick complex of French Second Empire styling was situated on 86 acres on the east side of Middlefield Road. Once the Ravenswood property of I.C. Woods, it was donated to the church by Kate Johnson.

St. Patrick's ordained its first priests in 1900. At least during the first 75 years of the century, Menlo Park was the common bond between priests throughout Western America. The institution's list of graduates reads like a Who's Who in Western Catholicism. It includes one cardinal, at least seven archbishops and more than 30 bishops. By 1974, the year of the seminary's Diamond Jubilee, of 14 dioceses in three states, all but two were headed by men from Menlo Park.

The Menlo Park brotherhood dominated the hierarchy of the Roman Catholic Church in the American West.

Graduates reported that education at St. Patrick's was "military and impersonal." Traditionally, books, magazines and newspapers, except those specifically authorized, were strictly forbidden. Correspondence, other than with immediate relatives, was not allowed. Food packages were confiscated. Attrition was high. In one class, of 48 seminarians who began, only seven were ordained 12 years later.

Giovanni (John) Beltramo's boarding house on Glenwood Avenue housed numerous newly-arrived Italians who found work on the great estates.

ITALIANS OF MENLO PARK

Menlo Park had a budding Italian community by the last years of the nineteenth century. Most were from the Piedmont and Lombardy area of northwest Italy near the borders of Switzerland and France. Many had learned gardening at home, working in farming communities. Amedeo Gado, who arrived in Menlo Park in 1926 and became grounds superintendent at the Leon F. Douglass estate, states that "many of the beautiful gardens of the area owe their existence to the horticultural skills of Italian immigrants." Piedmontese, an Italian dialect, was commonly spoken in the gardens of Menlo Park.

When there was a position to fill, superintendents sought the assistance of John Beltramo. For newly arriving Italians, the first stop on the Peninsula was Beltramo's large boarding house located on what became Glenwood Avenue between Middlefield Road and El Camino Real. Beltramo also maintained a small vineyard where he grew Muscat grapes. While awaiting permanent employment, immigrants worked the Beltramo vineyard.

John Beltramo was legendary among the new arrivals. He provided workers good food and many comforts of home as long as they adhered strictly to his codes of ethical conduct. He tolerated neither vulgarity nor brawling. Any man caught even talking to a Beltramo daughter was kicked out of the house.

Beltramo provided shelter and jobs for untold numbers of Italians. He was photographed in his vineyard where he grew muscat grapes.

Amedeo Gado, grounds superintendent at Victoria Manor, relied on Beltramo to provide gardeners. Here Gado was photographed with his bride, Rita Ardizzoia, May 26, 1938.

Billy Beltramo, a distant cousin of Giovanni, worked as a driver for San Francisco Archbishop William Patrick Riordan. Here he awaits the archbishop in front of St. Patrick's Seminary.

MENLO PARK IN 1898

Until the twentieth century, Menlo Park was primarily a summer place for San Francisco's fashionable elite. Most arrived in late spring and were gone before the end of summer.

But there were permanent residents there as well. According to the San Mateo County Great Register for 1898, there were 247 voters in Menlo Park. They represented 26 different states and 13 foreign countries. Sixty-eight had been born in California, 55 in Ireland, 14 in the state of New York, and nine each in England and Sweden. The smattering of others created no trend.

There were 56 farmers, followed by laborers, gardeners and carpenters. The list included seven coachmen, six blacksmiths, four teamsters, three hotel men and four who claimed to be capitalists. Two are listed as druggists, two as liquor dealers, one was a saloon keeper, one clergyman, one dentist and one doctor. Eighteen other types of employment were listed on the voting register. Such figures are at least partially misleading. This was a period of universal male suffrage; women weren't counted.

Blacksmithing was still a dominant town business in 1898.

Louise Tevis Sharon

Frederick William Sharon

Sharon was son of U.S. Senator William Sharon. His marriage to Louise Tevis combined two of the West's great fortunes.

FREDERICK W. SHARON

Frederick W. Sharon (1859-1915) was the scion of Nevada Senator William Sharon (1820-1885), an unscrupulous Comstock millionaire and one of San Francisco's richest men. Young Sharon married well. He went to the altar (1884) with Louise Tevis Breckinridge, a charming albeit cunning young San Francisco woman of brilliant accomplishments. Shortly after the nuptials, the Sharons headed for Paris, where they established a home and lived for 20 years. Their appearances in San Francisco were rare and always the occasions for much celebration.

Few San Franciscans so thoroughly immersed themselves in the international social whirl or so completely understood the fine and exhausting art of entertainment. While in Paris, seeking surcease from the constant demands upon their time, both Fred and Louise Sharon took to using cocaine, society's drug of choice during the 1890s. She eventually came to see the practice as "a filthy habit" and gave it up. He never did. It was believed that cocaine contributed to his early death.

Sharon died while residing at the family-owned Palace Hotel in San Francisco. Due to his early passing, an enormous house planned for the heights above Menlo Park was never built. Only a "cottage" had been erected on the property. Sharon's widow attached little sentimentality either to San Francisco or the Peninsula. After 1915, she closed the Menlo Park cottage and returned to Paris.

MENLO PARK HISTORICAL ASSOCIATION

This 32-room home on Sharon Heights, often acclaimed as the Sharon mansion, was merely "the cottage." The planned big house was never built.

SHOWPLACE IN THE HILLS

Frederick W. Sharon and his wife had spent 20 years living in cosmopolitan Paris. After the earthquake and fire that ripped San Francisco in 1906, they returned to supervise reconstruction of damaged family holdings. They rented a home on Pacific Avenue in San Francisco.

But sprawling Peninsula estates were considered chic for the California rich and the Sharons would be satisfied with nothing less. As early as 1887, Sharon had begun purchasing property in the hills above Menlo Park. Now the couple chose a dominating 600-acre site on the hill for a palatial country seat. The property was bounded north and south by Walsh and Sand Hill roads.

Architect George Kelham, brought west by Sharon to design the new Palace Hotel, was commissioned to plan the Peninsula house. He first designed a 32-room redwood-shingled structure that Sharon referred to as "a cozy cottage." Although the main house was never built, the cottage on Sharon Heights became a California showplace. It was surrounded by a massive wrought-iron fence. Millions were poured into construction and property development.

With a commanding view of the bay and surrounding country, the cottage was celebrated for an elaborate ballroom and oriental billiard room. Chambers were decorated with tapestries and other art treasures that the Sharons had acquired in Europe. Weekend visitors, greeted by a staff of eight butlers, were provided hand-lettered menus from which to make meal choices. Dinners, strictly formal, featured eight to twelve courses.

Holland tulips were brought by the shipload. Japanese cherry trees bloomed around an artificial lake. There were daffodils in profusion and 40 acres of fruit orchards. Fifteen miles of graveled roads were bordered by meticulously manicured lawns.

MENLO PARK, CALIFORNIA: BEYOND *the* GATE

Menlo Country Club was built on the north side of Woodside Road.

+2

68 # MENLO COUNTRY CLUB

Historians argue about where the golfing craze started. Most agree that the original American course of import was St. Andrews, at Yonkers, New York, in 1888. The sport intrigued wealthy Peninsulans. At the Burlingame Country Club (established in 1893), a nine-hole course was in use by 1900 and an 18-hole course by 1912.

Success bred success. Fashionable Menlo Park residents informally established the Menlo Golf and Country Club in 1900. *Almendral*, the old Selby property fronting on County Road bounded by Selby Lane and Atherton Avenue, was the first venue. One feature of the grounds had been a half-mile-long oval where sulky races were held. Thereon, members constructed a nine-hole golf course, crossing the oval four times. Hazards were existing fences and trees.

When Selby heirs expressed a wish to sell the land, members incorporated, September 23, 1909, as the Menlo Country Club. They began seeking a new facility and the following year purchased 120 acres on the north side of Woodside Road. Initially they installed a nine-hole golf course and a temporary clubhouse. Members announced an intent to build the most luxurious facility on the Peninsula. In 1911, their 18-hole course was completed and in May 1912, "everybody claiming membership in Peninsula society" was present for the housewarming of the new clubhouse.

Members of the Menlo Country Club gathered on the golf course. Competitions with the Burlingame Club were fierce.

Many of the Peninsula social elite belonged to both the Burlingame and Menlo clubs. But animosity soon developed when those from Burlingame came to perceive that Menlo Park was attempting to steal their social thunder.

MENLO PARK HISTORICAL ASSOCIATION

Senator Samuel Shortridge

CALIFORNIA'S SILVER-TONGUED ORATOR

"Bespectacled, balding and bug-eyed," is how one neighbor described Samuel M. Shortridge (1861-1952) who was elected to the U.S. Senate in 1920. No local resident was better known for his oratorical skill. He was earnest but not excitable, fervid but not fiery, a genuine "Henry Clay of the Pacific." Other admirers referred to him as "the Cicero of California," comparing him to the Roman orator who had been the great master of diction, gestures and Latin prose.

Attorneys dreaded meeting Shortridge in court because of his masterly skill swaying judges and juries. His summations were models of beauty and eloquence. For decades, he was the chosen local voice of the Republican Party. "Where Shortridge speaks, Republican majorities grow." He eulogized President McKinley upon his assassination and waved the banner for William Howard Taft. His oratory bristled with Americanism and love of country.

Shortridge thirsted to wear the toga of a U.S. Senator. Largely out of gratitude for past services, he was nominated in 1920 and rode into office for the first of two six-year terms on a wave of post-World War I isolationism. He delighted telling audiences that during his first campaign he delivered 98 speeches visiting 83 cities in 19 counties. Cost of the campaign was $672. And, so he said, "I never kissed a baby." Shortridge's home, a wisteria-covered New England Colonial built in 1899, was on Elena Avenue at Park Lane. The house's only renovation was for the impending visit of President Warren G. Harding in 1923. That visitation never occurred because of Harding's untimely death. The home was in Menlo Park when he was elected. By the time he left office, it was in the new town of Atherton.

A photographer snapped Shortridge on the steps of his Elena Avenue home.

RICHARD AND PEGGY BUCKLEY

Few Peninsula communities became better known for their much-fabled outdoor weddings.

A STUNNING MRS. MURPHY

"Very beautiful, very elaborate and altogether swagger," just what everyone expected for the wedding of pretty Frances Sherwood Hopkins to dry goods heir Eugene Murphy. The dimpled bride, a favorite of Menlo Park high society, was grandniece of railroading millionaire Mark Hopkins and niece of Edward Whiting Hopkins.

Guests from up and down the Peninsula gathered on the oak-studded lawn at the Menlo Park home of the bride's sister, Mrs. Warren D. Clark, June 20, 1903, to witness the ceremony performed on the wide, flower bedecked veranda. The wedding procession emerged from the house precisely at noon. Accompanied by her uncle, Frances passed down a miniature aisle formed by ribbons drawn through hoops of flowers held by six little children. Her long veil and splendid gown of white liberty satin, lavishly trimmed with quantities of rare ancestral Duchess lace, generated sighs of delight.

"Absolutely fabulous," cooed San Francisco's social czar Ned Greenway, who always evaluated such events. Social scribes were hard pressed to find adequate superlatives to describe it. But all were effervescent in their praise of the charming bride, who, they unanimously agreed, was both glowingly radiant and stunningly beautiful.

Mr. and Mrs. Eugene Murphy, seen leaving for their honeymoon at Del Monte in 1903.

The earthquake of 1906 prompted construction of this massive house by Pauline Payne.

PAULINE PAYNE BUILT A HOUSE TO LAST

In 1880, Pauline O'Brien, niece of silver king William O'Brien, married Theodore Fryatt Payne (1845-1907), proprietor of the Payne Bolt Works of San Francisco. The pair acquired 55 verdant acres at Menlo Park in a delightful location along Valparaiso Avenue west of El Camino Real.

Theodore Payne died before construction of the new house began. On the property, Mrs. Payne ordered the erection of a substantial Italian-style villa. Having survived the earthquake of 1906, she wanted a home solid enough to withstand the most severe California temblor.

Spacious interiors required furnishing on an especially grand scale.

Mrs. Payne demanded the best of everything. Design of this house was unique; there were eight master bedroom suites. The lady expected all of her grown children along with their spouses to move in with her. None ever did.

The massive 52-room structure, costing more than a million dollars, became a topic of considerable curiosity; it was the first home west of the Mississippi constructed of poured concrete and reinforcing steel. Creating the mold required so much lumber that later the wood was used to build several normal-sized Menlo Park houses.

During the period of construction, Mrs. Payne foraged Europe for furniture and statuary she felt essential for decoration of the house and garden. Interiors were unsurpassed. Floors were hardwood parquet. Fireplaces, mantles and the grand stairway were done in Italian marble. Halls were highlighted with imported wood paneling.

Mrs. Joseph A. Donohoe presented St. Joseph's School to the children of the town.

ST. JOSEPH'S SCHOOL

Most of the children in Menlo Park at the turn of the century were Roman Catholic of Irish or Italian descent. Recognizing the need for a parochial school, Mrs. Joseph A. Donohoe deeded five acres of property adjacent to the Convent of the Sacred Heart for the construction of a grammar school "for the village children...." St. Joseph's, as the school was known, was named for her late banker husband.

The Mesdames of the Sacred Heart agreed to provide teaching services. St. Joseph's School, a tuition-free institution, opened with four classrooms for 74 boys and girls of modest means in the fall of 1906. Margherita Ardizzoia (Gado), who attended during the 1920s, felt the education was equal to what the girls at the Convent received. "We were provided with everything, even pencils and paper."

Famed in the annals of St. Joseph's is the story of Mother Mary Foley who became principal a few months after the school opened. She ruled "like a general" until retirement in 1949. Old-timers delight recounting the tale of a black airedale, "Marco Polo," who used to follow his mistress, Tappy Kimball, to school every day. When Tappy graduated, Mother Foley bestowed a diploma on Marco Polo for his eight years of perfect attendance.

Mother Mary Foley acted as principal of St. Joseph's from 1906 to 1949.

A railroad crossing of the Bay was completed in 1907.

RAILROAD ACROSS THE BAY

Dumbarton Point, near the East Bay town of Newark, had long attracted the attention of nineteenth-century transportation specialists who viewed the location as ideal for construction of a railroad bridge. From Dumbarton Point to the West Shore near Menlo Park was a scant 1,500 feet. Water was a mere 50 feet deep. After protracted haggling, a three-year construction project began in 1907.

Advantages of such a crossing seemed clear. Rail distance between Oakland and San Francisco would be cut by 26 miles, an estimated 40 minutes. Furthermore, the high cost of rerouting freight via Southern Pacific ferryboats would be eliminated. Completion of the line was expected to stimulate Peninsula business and industrial activity.

Total length of the steel structure, counting a 310-foot, 1,500-ton center lift span and six 180-foot, 500-ton side spans, anchored to double reinforced concrete piers, was 1,390 feet. In the lift position, clearance was 70 feet at the high water mark. The "stupendous structure of steel," completed in September 1910 at a cost of $3.5 million, was a remarkable piece of engineering. A major celebration was staged in Newark, September 24, 1910, when the first train steamed across.

The last freight train crossed the bridge in 1982.

Dumbarton Bridge spanned the narrowest section of the South Bay.

Oakmeadows, a heavy-timbered and gabled house, was built for Abraham Stern in 1910.

JEWISH FAMILIES OF MENLO PARK

After the 1906 earthquake, many of the San Francisco's most prominent Jewish families joined the exodus to the Peninsula. Among them were the nephews of millionaire garment maker Levi Strauss. Abraham, Jacob and Sigmund Stern each acquired 20 Menlo Park acres upon which they built marvelous summer homes with adjoining gardens. Abraham's *Oakmeadows*, built in 1910, was a 30-room Tudor mansion designed by architect Houghton Sawyer. The impressive, heavy-timbered and gabled home was at 47 Stern Lane.

Equally elegant, albeit apparently unnamed, were Jacob's and Sigmund's mansions along Atherton Avenue. Each nephew expended a quarter of a million dollars on development.

In 1913, when Abraham Stern died, *Oakmeadows* was purchased by Emanuel S. Heller, brother-in-law of banking magnate I.W. Hellman. The Hellers, with the critical assistance of architect Willis Polk, added a study paneled in eucalyptus, and a baronial dining room with imported furnishings and paneling dating back to the sixteenth century. Formal gardens were planned by John McLaren. Clara Hellman Heller called the house *La Robleda*.

Not far away, in 1907, on a six-acre spread at 420 Selby Lane, Louis and Lucie Stern erected *Byde a Whyle*. This home, the epitome of gracious living, was especially known for its beautiful landscaping with sunken garden, swimming pool and fruit trees. Louis' widow lived there until her death. This estate was subdivided in the 1970s.

Sigmund Stern, favorite nephew of San Francisco clothing manufacture Levi Strauss, was photographed in Menlo Park with his wife Rosalie and daughter Elise. Elise later became Mrs. Walter A. Hass.

⑦ AN ONGOING TRADITION

Unlike many representatives of the Menlo Park elite who seemed firmly committed to principles of self-aggrandizement, many German Jewish families adhered to their tradition that those who achieved financial success had a responsibility to give something back to the communities in which they lived.

Sigmund and Rosalie Stern built a rather formal home surrounded by formal gardens on Atherton Avenue west of Selby Lane. The house, completed in 1908, had one of the earliest swimming pools on the Peninsula.

During World War I, not only did Rosalie Stern lead the effort to transform the grounds of Camp Fremont base hospital into a garden wonderland, she converted her ballroom into an assembly area where Red Cross volunteers made surgical dressings. She and Clara Heller also opened their adjoining gardens for numerous picnics and barbecues, hosting hundreds of lonesome soldiers of Camp Fremont. After the armistice, these families brought thousands of convalescing veterans from Letterman Army Hospital to be entertained on their estates.

GEORGE M. BOWLES

This elegant structure, Ockley, *was the estate house of the J. Leroy Nickel family.*

J. LEROY NICKEL

The large wood house located on 25 acres on the east side of Middlefield Road not far from the entry to the James C. Flood estate was the J. Leroy Nickel home. He called the place *Ockley*.

Nickel (1851-1937) had married (1885) Nellie Sarah Miller (1865-1944), the only surviving child of the multi-million dollar German cattle baron Henry Miller (1827-1916). Upon the latter's death, the Pennsylvania-born Nickel, formerly a liquor merchant, ascended to the presidency of the Miller & Lux Company. The firm controlled water resources throughout the San Joaquin Valley, oil lands and the West's largest cattle herds.

As late as 1916, Mexican *vaqueros*, company employees, drove cattle herds from the San Joaquin Valley across Pacheco Pass to Gilroy and thence along the Peninsula to South San Francisco. Men rode ahead to announce a herd's approach. Menlo Park residents were cautioned to close gates, least shade-seeking animals wander into their shops and gardens. Cattle were driven along both El Camino Real and Middlefield Road, often within a few feet of Nickel's front door.

Originally a summer place and one of the first Menlo estates to be completely wired for electricity, *Ockley* became a year-round home during the Depression. There, Nickel maintained glass houses and a sizeable fruit orchard. Five acres were reserved for his prized chickens and game birds.

His four children remembered him as a strict disciplinarian who required them to take cold baths daily. If they didn't descend by 7 a.m., they received no breakfast.

Ockley, just north of Oak Grove Avenue, later sold for the Maple Manor development.

GEORGE M. BOWLES

J. Leroy Nickel

The family of San Francisco Mayor James Rolph Jr. was photographed at the Menlo Park depot.

JAMES ROLPH'S PENINSULA

Among the more popular and visible personalities of Menlo Park in the years prior to World War I, was San Francisco Mayor James Rolph Jr. (1861-1934). Rolph, the city's most successful politician, had been elected there in 1911 and re-elected in 1915, 1919, 1923 and 1927.

Between 1912 and 1915, Rolph rented *Holm Grove*, the Joseph A. Donohoe estate on Middlefield Road in Menlo Park where he brought his family to vacation. The entire family, especially Rolph and his three children, appear to have cherished their time in Menlo Park, away from the glare of public scrutiny.

Rolph found the Peninsula reminiscent of a bygone age.

Obviously relaxed, Mayor Rolph frolicked with his kids while vacationing on the Peninsula.

Stanford graduates held warm memories for Charlie Meyer's famed drinking spa, the scene of raucous entertainments.

A DRINKING SPA TO REMEMBER

Stanford students lamented the end to the era of beer and song in 1909 when a wave of reform started by university authorities swept into Menlo Park and the town's saloons were ordered padlocked.

Most legendary of all the drinking emporiums had been Charlie Meyer's, where the last stein was drained and the last name was carved in the proprietor's wood tables in June 1910. Always a favorite gathering spot for Stanford students, Meyer had opened a saloon at Mayfield in 1901. The tables, already scarred and carved (purchased from the previous owner), had been in use there since 1892.

Mayfield closed its saloons in 1906. Meyer picked up his kegs and migrated to Menlo Park, opening on the southeast corner of El Camino Real and Oak Grove Avenue.

Football victories and raucous fraternity initiations were religiously celebrated in Meyer's back room. University athletes, great and small, carved initials in the round tables, which students came to regard as objects of veneration. Upon closure in 1910, Stanford clubs in Los Angeles and San Francisco attempted to buy them. But Meyer offered the cherished relics to the university museum. The gift was refused because of its association with beer. David Starr Jordan, the university president declared: "I wish they were all chopped into kindling wood and I'd like to help do it."

After Meyer's closed, the tables disappeared. Sometime later, 15 scarred tabletops reappeared, acquired by Menlo liquor merchant Alexander Beltramo. As late as World War II, they were in use at the Oasis, Beltramo's beer hall and restaurant on El Camino Real near Cambridge Avenue. After Beltramo sold that business, several of the "sacred" relics were placed on display in his liquor store.

University President David Starr Jordan didn't share the same warm feelings for Meyer's saloon. He felt the place inimical to academic pursuits.

At first welcomed, Stanford students soon gained repute as a collective curse on the tranquility of the nearby town.

UNIVERSITY STUDENTS SEEN AS CURSE OF TOWN

While some residents painted Stanford students as "naive and innocent," townsfolk had long regarded university men as the worst curse that Menlo Park was forced to endure. After the turn of the century, students who frequented the town's numerous saloons were scrupulously avoided by residents. In 1908, one obviously drunk student had been shot and killed by a Menlo resident who had felt threatened.

The pastor at the Church of the Nativity complained that the usually inebriated university boys were dangerous to all women, girls and children. The San Francisco archbishop harangued the Stanford administration, branding students as "idle and vicious." He claimed that the young ladies at the Convent of the Sacred Heart and the boys of St. Patrick's Seminary were being continually harassed and insulted.

"We cannot educate men and have saloons taking part in their education," declared angry Stanford President David Starr Jordan. A vigorous campaign was launched to close Menlo saloons. University authorities ultimately succeeded. In 1909, a law was enacted making it illegal to sell alcoholic beverages within 1.5 miles of the campus. Saloon keepers were enraged.

Hahn renamed Petite
Forêt *for his wife, calling
the estate* Fennwood.

PHOTOGRAPHER AS HISTORIAN

During the early years of the twentieth century, Albert George Charles Hahn (1858-1935), one of the premier photographers of that day, became the owner of *Petite Forêt*, built originally for Captain Charles Goodall. Hahn renamed the Glenwood Avenue residence *Fennwood* in honor of his wife, the former Harriet Rose Fenn.

Before the Panama-Pacific International Exposition in 1915, at the behest of Hillsborough millionaire Henry P. Bowie, who was art director for the San Francisco event, Hahn set out with his camera to create the San Mateo County exhibit, a collection of lantern slides to reveal the hidden wonders of the Peninsula.

He recorded 273 images on four-by-four-inch glass plates, which he meticulously hand-colored. The stunning photos were so perfectly painted that, in 1998, when the plates were rediscovered in the attic of *Fennwood*, professional photographers erroneously believed that Hahn had used some form of early color plate.

At the Exposition, this collection gave San Mateo County life and color that few people had ever seen before.

Harriet Rose Fenn Hahn

A.G.C. Hahn

The cadets of William Warren School lined up in dress uniforms for a group photograph.

WILLIAM WARREN SCHOOL

Today Menlo Park is known for its outstanding private schools. One from early in the century was the William Warren School, founded in 1915 by Easterner William Herbert Warren. The school, for grades one through eight, was situated on the old Fife estate on Alejandra Avenue and the County Road. The first year, there were just 13 students. Every year thereafter, another grade was added until ultimately all 12 grades were being taught. Two students constituted the first graduating class in 1920.

Warren operated the institution under military discipline. Boys at the boarding school were uniformed in West Point gray. They awakened to the sound of bugles, marched to class and practiced techniques of marksmanship at the rifle range. Rule breakers were harshly treated. Penalties included running in formation until exhausted; five-hour marches weren't uncommon.

The original campus was situated on 12 landscaped acres including vegetable gardens and fruit orchards. Cadets were required to work the gardens as their primary form of exercise; sporting activities were secondary.

Warren remained headmaster until 1924, when he was replaced by Clifford Dennis who incorporated the institution and, to the delight of students, eradicated the school's military character.

Thereafter, the name of the institution was changed to Menlo School for Boys.

Students didn't take especially well to the military discipline imposed by Warren. Cadets Bob Girvin (left) and Ray Ehrman appear more relaxed than the headmaster would have preferred.

Soldiers at Camp Fremont lived in tent cities.

CAMP FREMONT

"Here we are at Camp Fremont, where real men and real soldiers are being made," wrote Harry C. Freeman from Menlo Park in 1917. "You folks...should see the camp for yourselves to really appreciate the beautiful health and nature spot it is."

Of 16 new basic training centers designated by the War Department to prepare soldiers for the Western Front, Camp Fremont was the largest west of the Mississippi. It encompassed 25,000 acres, almost 15 square miles. The main part of the base spread from El Camino Real to Alameda de las Pulgas and from Valparaiso Avenue south to San Francisquito Creek, surrounding the downtown area. Practice maneuvers were undertaken in both San Mateo and Santa Clara counties, extending onto university property, west to Woodside and Portola Valley and into the watershed.

Few World War I recruits were as comfortable in basic training.

Construction of 1,124 temporary buildings began in July 1917. No wooden barracks were erected. Men, six in each, lived in canvas tents with wooden floors and side walls. This tent city covered more than 1,000 acres.

Menlo Park was chosen as a training facility because of the similarity of its terrain to the battlefields of France. In the hills west of town, trainees built foxholes and dug trenches while practicing crawling under barbed wire and lobbing hand grenades across the open landscape. The temperate climate permitted year-round training.

Trainees brought the town to life. It quickly took on the appearance of a bustling Gold Rush mining community. Vacant stores were purchased or rented. The Army built a 3,500-book library, a 1,000-seat theater, two baseball diamonds and two football fields, one with a 10,000-seat grandstand.

Introduction of poison gas during World War I forever altered the future course of military training.

HILLS ECHOED WITH EXPLOSIONS

Training at Camp Fremont was conducted on the assumption that the soldiers might be sent into battle immediately. Recruits trained with Springfield bolt-action rifles and carried 16-inch bayonets. Firing ranges in the hills west of the town were the largest in the nation. There were 800 targets at distances varying from 100 to 1,000 yards. By 1918, trainees were firing two million rounds of ammunition every month. Town residents became oblivious to the around-the-clock rattling of machine guns.

Artillery pounded away at unseen targets and the hills reverberated with the blasts of explosive shells. After closure of Camp Fremont, when the hills were opened to development, salvage teams sifted more than a million pounds of lead from the soil; 400,000 pounds were picked up in Sharon Heights alone.

The camp was ordered to begin closing down immediately after the armistice in November 1918. The order did not become official until September 1919, when the last three men of the one-time garrison of 43,000 were sent to San Francisco stations.

Training emphasized the realities of the Western Front. Skill with a bayonet was thought essential for the vicious fighting associated with trench warfare.

Arrival of the soldiers brought downtown Menlo Park to life.

HUB OF PENINSULA SOCIAL ACTIVITIES

Many of the Peninsula's most fashionable families entertained soldiers of Camp Fremont. The July 4, 1918, garden party at the Hillsborough estate of George Pope was especially grand.

On weekends, Camp Fremont trainees crowded the streets of Menlo Park and Palo Alto. Jitneys zipped between the camp and Redwood City, the closest place alcoholic beverages could be obtained. An electric trolley linked Palo Alto and San Jose. The round trip was 50 cents. Few soldiers could afford the $1.20 rail fare to San Francisco.

Officers looked forward to weekend parties along the Peninsula. The George Popes of Hillsborough brought hundreds up the Peninsula by special train in 1918 for a July Fourth barbecue and garden party.

There were dances on the lawn of Gardener Nerve Sanitorium in Belmont and at San Mateo's fashionable Peninsula Hotel. In Redwood City, the Native Daughters of the Golden West staged a dance on the front lawn of the courthouse. During summer, trainees crowded the swimming beach at San Mateo's Coyote Point.

Hardly had the camp opened when military officials noted an unusually large influx of women into the area. At least three were arrested after it was determined that each had acquired three husbands. Camp hospital nurses were off-limits to enlisted personnel. One private was sentenced to 30 days in the guardhouse for accompanying a nurse to a movie. Surprise was registered after the camp closed because of the number of marriages between former nurses and enlisted men.

Hostess House at the camp attracted soldiers and girls from the surrounding community. Moved after the war, the structure is presently MacArthur Park, a restaurant in Palo Alto.

Highest standards maintained at Camp Fremont

War Department officials assured American parents that everything was being done to maintain the highest standards of morality among trainees at Camp Fremont. They created a five-mile zone around the cantonment where the sale of alcoholic beverages was prohibited.

Dr. John M. Stillman, acting president of Stanford University, was infuriated. Objecting to the location of Fremont's tent city, he anguished that the presence of these virile young men in proximity with the university's comely coeds might have a disastrous effect on the morals of the community. "Shame on you, Stillman," editorialized a local newspaper. "Either he has little confidence in the moral sense of Stanford coeds or has a mighty poor opinion of men who wear the uniform of the United States soldier."

Guards were posted to assure that trainees did not invade the Stanford campus and that comely coeds didn't infiltrate the military camp.

Nevertheless, when the fall semester 1917 began, two companies of soldiers were assigned to "watch and guard" the coeds, to assure that no soldiers invaded Stanford lines and that no coeds surreptitiously infiltrated Fremont's tent city. There was tremendous competition among the military units for this assignment.

Schumann-Heink as Marie in the "Flying Dutchman"

Schumann-Heink as Ortrud in "Lohengrin"

ERNESTINE SCHUMANN-HEINK

The German-born diva became a naturalized American citizen and offered her loyalty to the Allied cause during World War I.

For four decades, the name of Madame Schumann-Heink (1861-1936) was known throughout America. Born in Bohemia and trained in Europe, by the time she made her first trip to America in 1898, she was already a renowned singer.

For years, she performed with the New York Metropolitan Opera Company, mastering more than 150 roles. In 1903, she began a two-year, 40,000-mile tour of the United States. "No artist has ever appeared in the city that earned and received the ovations tended this superb woman...," wrote a San Francisco critic after her appearance in April 1904.

Schumann-Heink developed a lifelong love affair with the United States. She became a citizen in 1905 and, the following year, brought her eight children to America. After the outbreak of World War I, her eldest son returned to Germany. He became a submarine commander and was lost at sea. Two other sons served in the American Army and battled Germans on the Western Front; another joined the U.S. Navy. When the United States entered the war, the renowned diva offered her loyalty to the government. She made history May 15, 1918, singing at Camp Dix, New Jersey, to 50,000 soldiers awaiting transportation to France. Following the war, she toured the United States and Europe, singing in military hospitals for the thousands who had been maimed and wounded during the struggle.

"SOLDIERS' MOTHER" SINGS AT STANFORD

Stanford Stadium, June 9, 1918, witnessed the "greatest military spectacle" ever staged in California when the internationally acclaimed contralto Ernestine Schumann-Heink appeared to raise money for the soldiers of Camp Fremont.

Special trains brought 15,000 flag-toting soldiers from all over Northern California. Regiment after regiment marched into the stadium for the mammoth patriotic song festival. With a decided German accent, Schumann-Heink sang with 10,000 Camp Fremont soldiers. Another 1,000 civilians from Menlo Park and other Peninsula communities added to the chorus.

Schumann-Heink was looked upon as one of America's most patriotic women. By the time of her appearance at Stanford stadium, she was commonly called "the Soldiers' Mother."

During her long career, Schumann-Heink performed for presidents, emperors and queens. But she was most at home with soldiers. "I can honestly say that I think my voice has given more happiness to the soldiers, and given me more happiness in singing for them, than I ever got out of my greatest opera and concert days."

Fifteen thousand soldiers marched into Stanford Stadium to engage in a patriotic songfest with Schumann-Heink.

Americans commonly referred to the great diva as "the Soldiers' mother."

Assignment to the Camp Fremont base hospital was considered both light and pleasant duty.

MENLO PARK HISTORICAL ASSOCIATION

CAMP FREMONT'S HEALTHY ENVIRONMENT

Army commanders were inordinately proud of Camp Fremont's healthy environment. "It is absolutely free of epidemics," reported a headquarters document in March 1918. At that time, there were 15,000 men in training and, during a two-month period, only 237 contagious patients had been admitted to the hospital. Most were cases of measles and mumps.

Construction of the $500,000 hospital complex began in 1917. The facility, three miles east of Menlo Park, was on 90 acres of former dairy land near Bayshore along Willow Road. While a few hospital buildings were two stories, most were single. All structures were connected by boardwalks. Wards were lettered from "A" to "Z" and had about 70 beds in each.

Although completely "off-limits" to trainees, nurses were some of the most popular personalities at the camp.

MENLO PARK HISTORICAL ASSOCIATION

Menlo Park social matron and philanthropist Rosalie Meyer Stern, wife of Levi Strauss executive Sigmund Stern, took it upon herself to beautify hospital grounds. She brought in landscape architect John McLaren to supervise the general scheme. Few landscaping projects were better executed. Members of the Peninsula social elite who belonged to the hospital's garden committee sent personal gardeners to participate in planting. On the hospital grounds, a 3,000-seat Garden Theater was erected. Convalescing patients attended free movies twice each week. Other days, there were singers. On weekends, regimental bands played while soldiers sang patriotic songs.

An outbreak of Spanish influenza resulted in the camp's quarantine in October 1918.

MEDICAL CRISIS AT CAMP FREMONT

Camp Fremont hospital nurses wrote of near idyllic conditions at the base hospital. Although wards filled with returning wounded, the daily sick list was the shortest of any training camp in the nation.

Off-duty nurses rode horseback along tree-lined, winding roads, often traversing the great estates. One wrote her family about the beauty of the Peninsula, noting that some of the roads around the camp were lined for miles with hydrangeas.

World War I was almost at an end when the first case of Spanish influenza was identified at Camp Fremont in 1918. On October 7, the camp was quarantined. Military policemen surrounded the base and visitors were turned away. The hustle of cars along Santa Cruz Avenue ceased. Gone were the gaily colored dresses and bright parasols. Soldiers wore flu masks to prevent the spread of the contagion. Hourly, ambulances filled with patients left the camp for the base hospital. One morning a regimental colonel, a supply sergeant, a battalion sergeant-major and a supply officer were all stricken.

The hospital was thrown into disarray. Assigned personnel were too few in number to handle the influx of flu victims. Wards bulged with patients, many delirious. Within 10 days of the outbreak, 1,800 victims, including 35 nurses stricken while providing care, filled the hospital.

One exhausted nurse, writing from the depths of depression, told her parents that "our prettiest and jolliest nurse," along with seven men on her ward passed away the same day.

Soldiers, wearing masks to protect them from the contagion, marched along University Avenue in Palo Alto.

Upon arrival in Siberia, soldiers trained at Menlo Park paraded in Vladivostok.

CAMP FREMONT'S BEST SENT TO SIBERIA

Soldiers at Camp Fremont were unprepared for what was about to happen. Khaki uniforms were exchanged for wool. Ankle-length buffalo-skin coats were added to each man's equipment. Troop trains rolled out of Menlo Park August 14, 1918. Shades in the cars were drawn. Trains were switched onto the Embarcadero in San Francisco and rolled directly to the docks at Fort Mason.

Five thousand men from Camp Fremont, trained for war in Europe, were being sent to participate (with 14 other nations) in an intervention in Siberia. A sense of foreboding descended upon soldiers who envisioned a barren icebound land of interminable snows. This was the start of one of the war's most ill-fated expeditions. Americans were landed at Vladivostok, September 2, 1918. The city was a cesspool. Buildings where the soldiers were berthed were cockroach-infested, lacked heat and had no working sanitary facilities.

World War I ended in November 1918, but Americans remained in Siberia until April 1920. Estimates of the number killed in the occupation ran as high as 300. Scores more died from plague, typhus, typhoid and scarlet fever. Thousands suffered from frostbite, malignant sore throats, and other weather-related maladies.

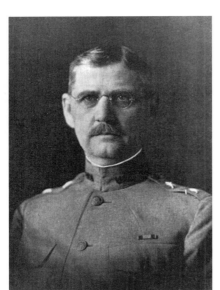

General William S. Graves, commander of forces in Siberia, admitted he did not know why American soldiers had been sent.

The most revealing comment about the intervention was made later by American General William S. Graves. "Though I was in command of the U.S. troops sent to Siberia," he said, "I must admit I don't know what we were trying to do there."

AMERICA'S FORGOTTEN ARMY

A deteriorating political situation in Russia had become a major concern in the West. Russia was in the grip of civil war. Bolsheviks seized control in 1917. A few months later the Russians made a separate peace with Germany.

Some U.S. government officials claimed that Americans were sent to Siberia to protect the Trans-Siberian Railroad and safeguard military supplies previously sent to Vladivostok. The new Soviet government was embarrassed by the intervention and subsequently claimed that it was an attempt to discredit the Bolshevik revolution and bring about a collapse of the state. Soldiers, trained at Camp Fremont, found conditions excruciating. In fall and spring, unpaved roads around Vladivostok became quagmires of fathomless mud. Winter temperatures plummeted to 60-75 degrees below zero.

"Fremont's Best" guarded bridges and depots along the Trans-Siberian Railroad that they were ordered to see did not fall into Bolshevik hands.

While Camp Fremont was closed and disassembled after the armistice in Europe, thousands who trained there remained in Siberia. In late 1919, Menlo Park residents collected tons of tobacco, chocolates and plum puddings for the Siberian Christmas Cheer Fund.

This was America's forgotten army. It both embarked and returned without fanfare.

Trained on the Peninsula, U.S. soldiers were not prepared for the freezing weather of Siberia. Menlo Park residents sent tons of chocolate, plum puddings, and tobacco for Christmas in 1919.

Menlo Park's downtown bristled with saloons. Two of the largest, Meyer's and O'Keefe's, were on opposite corners.

ALCOHOL SEEN AS INALIENABLE RIGHT

Few Menlo Park residents had sympathy for drinking restrictions imposed by university authorities or for federal Prohibition of the 1920s. Many regarded drinking alcohol as an inalienable right.

"Speakeasies," illegal drinking resorts, proliferated throughout the county in open defiance of federal laws. At Menlo Park, illegal stills operated almost openly in every neighborhood; bootleggers brazenly carried on their trade.

County officials anguished about Menlo Park, where disabled American soldiers were being cared for at the U.S. Veterans Hospital. These men, along with "naive and innocent" students at the nearby university, seemed easy prey to the "poison peddled by bootleggers." War was waged against bootleggers and officials called on right-thinking citizens of Menlo Park to assist them in wiping out the "nefarious trade." Townsfolk did not respond enthusiastically.

Highlighting the magnitude of the crisis, in October 1924, a major speakeasy was raided on Santa Cruz Avenue. Thirty-six inebriates were arrested and a large supply of bootlegged liquor was confiscated.

In March 1927, Menlo Park liquor merchant Alexander Beltramo was arrested on charges of illegal possession of liquor when Prohibition agents discovered several hundred gallons of wine stashed in a North Fair Oaks barn owned by Beltramo. He was brought to trial. A jury, comprised of local residents, claimed that the prosecution never proved that Beltramo was owner of the contraband booze. The case was dismissed for lack of evidence.

WHISKIES, BRANDIES, GINS, RUM, BITTERS, CORDIALS, BEER, ETC.

JOHN BELTRAMO

WHOLESALE AND RETAIL LIQUOR DEALER

IMPORTED AND CALIFORNIA SPARKLING AND VINTAGE WINES

CHAMPAGNES

GLENWOOD AVE. AND MIDDLEFIELD ROAD
¾ MILE NORTH WEST FROM MENLO PARK DEPOT   MENLO PARK, CALIF.

John Beltramo was the town's leading liquor merchant before and after Prohibition. He also saw to it that during the 1920s, Menlo Park was not completely dry.

Following the armistice, Camp Fremont's base hospital was transformed into a Veterans Administration facility.

VETERANS ADMINISTRATION HOSPITAL

The Veterans Administration Hospital, located on 96 acres along Willow Road near the Bayshore Freeway in Menlo Park, traces its origin to World War I, when it was opened as the base hospital for nearby Camp Fremont.

After the war the Army transferred control of the facility to the U.S. Public Health Service. It was used for the treatment of veterans suffering from tuberculosis.

In 1922, the hospital became part of the U.S. Veterans Bureau. New construction was begun. Two years later, at a cost of $1.4 million, 21 modern structures were opened for veterans afflicted with neuropsychiatric illnesses. In August 1923, President Warren G. Harding, then in California, was slated to dedicate the facility. Engraved invitations were sent; however, Harding died in San Francisco shortly before the dedication.

By century's end, almost all of the original buildings had been destroyed, but two of the 1917 structures are still used, albeit not for patient care; one is the facility's paint shop.

This hospital was the government's only locked psychiatric facility in Northern California. Improved neuropsychiatric drugs developed in the 1960s altered the hospital's role. Multi-year admissions were usually reduced to a matter of days.

Ken Kesey, author of *One Flew Over the Cuckoo's Nest*, was employed on a locked night ward at Menlo Park in 1959 and 1960. Much of his novel had its origin at this hospital.

Corrective hydrotherapy of this variety was used for treatment of manic depressives and psychotics at the Veterans Administration Hospital as late as the 1940s. Thereafter, the procedure was supplanted with drugs and electric shock.

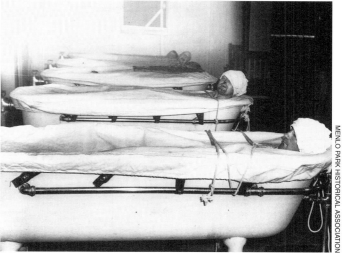

Leon Forest Douglass purchased the Payne house in 1921.

The Douglass family photographed in front of Victoria Manor, *as they called the great house.*

Famed tenor Enrico Caruso presented the inventor with this self-drawn cartoon.

INVENTOR MOVES TO MENLO PARK

One of the community's most celebrated residents was inventor Leon F. Douglass (1869-1940). For $600,000 in 1921, he purchased the 52-room Pauline Payne home, located on Valparaiso Avenue.

Douglass encountered his first phonograph in 1888 and immediately grasped its entertainment potential. He created and patented a coin-operated model. Almost immediately, the device was installed in dozens of public locations.

Douglass later patented a device for duplicating disc records by making a metal master from which flat, one-sided copies could be pressed. Sound quality was much improved.

In 1901, Douglass joined the Eldridge R. Johnson Company as vice-president and general manager. Dissatisfied with the business' name, Johnson assigned Douglass to come up with a new one. He chose the name Victor Talking Machine Company to honor his wife, the former Victoria Adams. The company pioneered many new recording techniques. Victor was the first company to record grand opera. Douglass signed the great tenor Enrico Caruso to make 10 records, promising, in 1903, to pay $400 each. The highest previous contract with a performer had been for $50 a song. Douglass later presented Caruso his first royalty check for $202,000.

Douglass theorized that householders didn't appreciate phonograph equipment topped with ungainly horns. In 1902, he patented a *Victrola* with the speaker and mechanism enclosed inside an elegant cabinet. It sold millions.

Following an emotional breakdown in 1905, Douglass moved to California and in 1921, to Menlo Park. The Payne home, which became both a residence and laboratory, he called *Victoria Manor*. There, he continued his experimentation.

Douglass' two daughters frequently participated in film experiments. Here they were filmed with a seal in the estate's swimming pool.

FILM INNOVATIONS TRACED TO MENLO PARK

Inventor Leon Douglass was mesmerized by motion pictures and experimented with film as early as 1912. His goal came to be the development of color movies, a process which he patented in 1912.

Douglass moved to Menlo Park in 1921, acquiring the massive home he called *Victoria Manor*. He turned the mezzanine and basement into his personal laboratories. During early years on the Peninsula, Douglass revolutionized film making, fashioning a remarkable new camera with a built-in triple scene dissolve, eliminating abrupt snapping from one scene to another, characteristic of early films.

His devices included combination and zoom lenses in addition to apparatuses for trick and unusual effects such as disappearing screen ghosts, shrinking of a single actor (though surrounded by normal-sized players) and the illusion of a person being engulfed in fire.

Underwater filming techniques became his passion and the swimming pool at *Victoria Manor* was his testing area. A window was cut in the pool's wall so that he could take movies from a vantage point inside an adjacent foxhole. The inventor's grandson, Earl Douglass Jr., remembers the day a convertible arrived at the house with a seal sitting in the back seat. "The seal plopped out...and waddled up to the pool as if he knew exactly what he was doing." The animal was filmed swimming underwater with the inventor's two daughters.

During his career, Douglass registered 50 patents, 24 of them while he was living at *Victoria Manor*.

Also a motion picture innovator, Douglass used his home as a laboratory.

Victoria Manor was festooned for the holiday when town youngsters were invited in for the annual Christmas party.

EARL DOUGLASS JR.

DOUGLASS BROUGHT CHRISTMAS CHEER TO MENLO

Menlo Park children never questioned the existence of Santa Claus. They knew that there was one and exactly who he really was. Santa was mild-mannered inventor Leon F. Douglass.

Though painfully shy, beginning in 1921, Douglass invited town children to attend what became annual Christmas Day parties at *Victoria Manor*. "My earliest memories of Douglass' house are the Christmas parties...always the highlight of the year," remarks Rita Gado, who grew up in town. "It was during the Depression...and going to the party was the best thing that could happen to a poor kid." Children assembled on the lawn facing the porch. Gardens were decorated. The mansion was festooned with garlands of evergreen. Christmas wreaths hung from second floor balconies.

MENLO PARK HISTORICAL ASSOCIATION

Santa's arrival was always much anticipated by the children.

One year Santa came in a small car, another in a limousine. Some claim he once flew in by airplane. Children remember Santa on the roof of the house. All presumed he descended the chimney; in fact, he ducked inside and came down an elevator. "We knew it was Mr. Douglass," states Gado. But it wasn't. The honor of impersonating Santa went to a man of the village. The inventor watched festivities from a second floor balcony. Girls received storybooks or beautiful dolls; boys got footballs, bats, balls, and mitts.

Parties ceased in 1934.

French Laundry

Helen Musso of Cupertino delights in telling tales of the Menlo French Laundry established by her grandparents, Pierre and Marie Larrecou, who brought their family to the Peninsula in 1893. It was located next to the grammar school at 1300 El Camino Real.

Until then, the patrician residents of the town's environs commonly sent their laces and linens to San Francisco or China for laundering. This changed with the arrival of the Larrecous. During the course of a century, the laundry has washed, starched and pressed the clothing and fine linens of the surrounding community. Since its establishment, the laundry has had five different proprietors and been relocated four times.

According to legend, the fame of the business dates from the late 1890s, when Jane Stanford, in preparation for a visit from President William McKinley, ordered a servant to send the tablecloth out to be laundered.

Naturally, she assumed that the magnificent hand-embroidered linen had been forwarded to New York as usual. In error, the servant had carted it off to the French Laundry in Menlo Park. At first irate, Mrs. Stanford was so pleased with the result that from that time forward all her laundry was done locally.

In 1945, Laurent and Eloise Lancestremere, longtime Menlo Park residents, purchased the business. They moved the operation to its present location at 558 Oak Grove Avenue in 1962. The laundry was acquired by Brent Edwards in 1990.

From the time of its establishment, proprietors have provided first-class service. Today, the laundry's fabric care specialist conducts seminars for Bay Area department stores on the proper care of delicate fabrics.

Patronage by Jane Stanford gave the French Laundry early credibility. The business is still existent. Note the Menlo Park gateway at the left.

The original Menlo Circus of 1920 was completely an enterprise of children.

ORIGIN OF THE MENLO PARK CIRCUS

It was incredibly simple and all started by three little girls in June 1920 who decided to put on a "summer circus." The idea was to help the sick children at the nearby Stanford Convalescent Home. The event was staged at the corner of Middlefield and Glenwood in Menlo Park. Neighbors were invited. The girls performed with two chickens, a cat, three dogs, a goat, a few ponies and a horse.

"Never again will there be quite such a circus as that one," declared Mrs. Albert Hahn, reminiscing years later. The girls raised $5.76. Beaming parents found the sum rather paltry and upped the ante. Thus the girls presented $500 to the convalescent home.

The circus idea took root. A year later at *Fennwood*, 42 children participated in "Menlo Park's Juvenile Circus." Each pony-mounted rider was clad in white breeches, red hunting coat and black velvet cap. Offspring of the Peninsula elite joined in. Among the performers were young Jimmy Flood, Peter McBean, Selah Chamberlain and Maxwell McNutt. Several thousand attended. Parents added booths reminiscent of county fairs.

So financially rewarding was this second circus that backers pledged to make it an annual event. The next, in 1922, was so successful that shortly thereafter 16 families united to form the Menlo Circus Club.

Louise Hahn was named "Queen Polly of the Circus" in 1922.

Berenice and Lurline Roth, daughters of Mr. and Mrs. William P. Roth, were elected "twin queens" of the Menlo Circus in 1925.

Menlo Circus Club

Men in white flannels and blue jackets and women in pastel coats with fox collars convened on March 21, 1923, for the formation of the Menlo Park Circus Club. Founders said it was "the only country club in America designed exclusively for children." Nineteen acres of the former Faxon D. Atherton estate located just behind the Sacred Heart Convent became club property.

June 23, 1923, the grounds at Menlo Park (now Atherton) opened for the first time as the "Children's Circus of Menlo Park." This inaugural event was a rousing success; 3,000 smart-setters turned out in their fashionable finery to appreciate the traditional events.

Annual circuses became increasingly sophisticated. In 1925, when 90 youngsters participated, Berenice and Lurline, twin daughters of Mr. and Mrs. William P. Roth, were elected "twin queens." Each vote cast required the purchase of a ticket. Thanks to friends and family, the Roth twins raised $17,000.

Old King Cole

The famed Menlo Park gate, erected in the 1850s, was destroyed by a speeding car in 1922.

GATEWAY WAS SYMBOLIC OF MENLO PARK

Dennis J. Oliver (1825-1886) and Daniel C. McGlynn married sisters. All hailed from Menlough, County Galway in Ireland. In 1852, Oliver and McGlynn purchased 1,700 acres on the Peninsula at the south end of the former *Rancho de las Pulgas.* Two years later they erected a dramatic arched wooden gateway marking a common driveway to their two homes. A sign on the arch read "Menlo Park." On either side of the main arch were smaller pedestrian entry gates, one bearing the name D.J. Oliver and the other D.C. McGlynn.

Before the railroad, this arched structure became a commonly recognized landmark. By 1863, tracks of the Peninsula railroad reached San Francisquito Creek and the local depot was erected opposite the Oliver-McGlynn gateway. Thus the stop became "Menlo Park."

In 1905, in an effort to preserve the famed landmark the estate of George C. Johnson gave the aging and already-rotting structure to the Menlo Parlor of the Native Sons of the Golden West. It stood until July 7, 1922, when it was struck by a speeding automobile and demolished.

Residents in the Fair Oaks (Atherton) district of Menlo Park had always seen themselves as having lived in an oasis of privilege.

AN OASIS OF PRIVILEGE

Most of Menlo Park's wealthiest families fancied themselves as having lived in the exclusive Fair Oaks neighborhood of the unincorporated town. In 1912, when they acquired a depot of their own, residents voted to call it Fair Oaks. This name, however, was opposed by the railroad because there already was such a station in Sacramento County. Thus people opted instead for the name Atherton.

Voters there in 1923 petitioned to become an incorporated town. They felt that this was the only way to assure that they would not be included within the boundaries of Menlo Park, where residents were seriously discussing incorporation on their own. The name chosen for the new entity was Atherton.

The boundary dividing Menlo Park and the new municipality was crooked and complex. Atherton and Menlo Park officials agreed to it only after heated debate. It was painstakingly drawn to assure that almost all of the huge landed estates became part of Atherton.

Atherton seceded from Menlo Park, incorporating on its own in 1923. Pictured is the Atherton (formerly Fair Oaks) station.

ATHERTON SECEDES FROM MENLO PARK

Menlo residents were talking about the possibility of incorporation, but a number of prominent families in the elegant Fair Oaks section chose not to be included. These residents, owners of the largest estates, petitioned the County Board of Supervisors in August 1923 asking that they be allowed to consider incorporating themselves. With an election the following month, Atherton became the eighth incorporated town in San Mateo County. Of 130 votes cast, 114 favored secession and the creation of a new town.

In the absence of a government center, Atherton's trustees met in the spacious parlor of the Clarence Walter mansion, causing one newspaper to comment that "it...is the most elaborate town hall this side of the North Pole." Dr. E.W. Westphal, a San Francisco dentist who owned one of the new town's larger homes, was made police chief. He pledged to keep Atherton's millionaire residents under control, rid the town of campers and eradicate hot dog stands that were beginning to clutter up Atherton's fair scenery.

Residents sought to preserve Atherton's rustic charm. Drives wound lazily among great oaks. A business section along El Camino Real was restricted to two blocks. Town founders were emphatic that there be no sidewalks.

Dumbarton Bridge opened in 1927. Eleanor Twohig, Miss San Francisco, was the first to cross.

DUMBARTON BRIDGE

Few things altered the life of Menlo Park more than the opening of Dumbarton Bridge, first automobile crossing of San Francisco Bay, January 15, 1927. The nine steel truss spans, approximately one mile in length and located in a direct line 25 miles southeast of San Francisco's Ferry Building, cost $2 million. One section lifted vertically between towers. This afforded ships a clearance of 135 feet and a clear channel with a width of 200 feet between fenders.

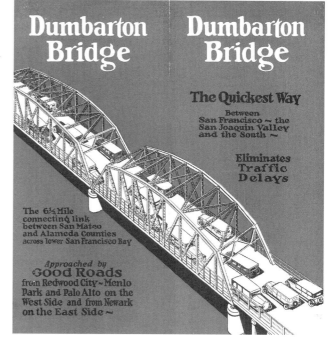

Promoters predicted a Peninsula population explosion. Menlo anxiously awaited new development and a promised economic boom.

But there was trouble. Three months after the opening, the bridge was closed by police because town exits were not available. A paving contractor could not complete work on Carlton Avenue because of recurring damage caused by premature bridge traffic. Willow Road leading to the bridge was still under construction.

On April 16, 1927, police officers were posted at both ends of the bridge to reroute traffic via Alviso. East Bay sports fans, headed for a Stanford track meet, became enraged. At the Menlo Park end, there was a near riot when disgruntled motorists broke through barriers. Some drivers cut across open fields to get to the bridge. The County Board of Supervisors stepped in. After three days, the barrier was broken. The bridge reopened on April 19, 1927, now on a 24-hour-a-day basis.

This structure lasted until 1984. It was destroyed by explosives when a new bridge replaced it that year.

By 1927, citizens of Menlo Park voted to incorporate.

El Camino Real is shown as it appeared in the 1930s.

Dr. Alfred E. Blake was the town's first mayor.

MENLO RESIDENTS RECOGNIZE ADVANTAGES OF INCORPORATION

Following Menlo Park's two-year period of incorporation, which ended in 1876, townsfolk had been adequately satisfied for their community to remain without official status.

But residents received a jolt in 1923 with the incorporation of neighboring Atherton. Thereafter, more and more effort in Menlo Park became directed toward its own incorporation. Champions called for sanitary laws to protect residents. Neglected streets were in hideous condition and needed improvement. Only with incorporation could the town establish a police force to end lawlessness.

One move to incorporate Menlo Park, in 1924, had been defeated by voters who questioned the ability of the town to exist as a viable entity on its own. By 1927, a couple of alternatives were under consideration. One, which won the approval of the Menlo Chamber of Commerce, was to seek annexation by Palo Alto. While recognizing advantages, Menlo Park attorneys agonized over the legality of a community overlapping county lines. The taxation question became muddled and the proposal was dropped.

A second alternative was to seek annexation by Atherton. This plan received support from the Menlo Park Merchants' Association, whose members pointed out that the management of Atherton was in the hands of successful businessmen who would see that affairs were carried out in the same efficient manner. A petition for incorporation was presented to Atherton trustees. Their response was icy.

Menlo voters finally decided to go it alone. That election, the most exciting in the town's history, was on November 15, 1927. Polls opened at 6 a.m. Vote counting wasn't completed until midnight. The incorporation was certified by the state and the date on the city seal is November 23, 1927.

The first meeting of the city council was held in the Masonic Hall on Tuesday evening December 6. Dr. A.E. Blake was the unanimous choice to become Menlo's first mayor.

Thomas Furman, formerly a tough San Francisco cop, became the town's first police chief.

Chief Furman posed with his daughter Dolores.

TOUGH COP LEADS NEW POLICE FORCE

Not long after incorporation in 1927, the town council offered the job of police chief to a legendary San Francisco cop, Thomas E. Furman. The smooth-shaven, heavyset Furman pinned on his chief's badge January 24, 1928.

During a brief tenure as chief, Furman left a lasting impression on the town of 2,000 inhabitants. After a single year in the position, he reported that 24 gambling dens had been closed down and 17 speakeasies padlocked.

There were no special thanks for the chief. In fact, his record resulted in a call for his ouster. Townsfolk believed his ardor was a threat to the prosperity of the town.

Given the man's previous reputation, his crusading zeal should have come as no surprise. Furman joined the San Francisco force in 1904 and, within a decade, had risen to the position of detective sergeant. He had been recognized for efficiency and integrity. He was considered one of San Francisco's most loyal and capable men. In 1914, Police Chief David A. White put Furman in charge of the White Slave Bureau, a squad of two men and five women. Furman learned that an endless number of girls, many as young as 13 and often runaways, had been lured into prostitution with drugs. His efforts saved the lives of countless young women.

The zealous Furman did not last long as Chief of Menlo Park Police. He was replaced in April 1930.

The new Corpus Christi Monastery as it appeared from Oak Grove Avenue.

Dominican Nuns of the Corpus Christi

A cloistered monastery for Dominican nuns, dream of the late San Francisco Archbishop Patrick William Riordan, had been long delayed by the earthquake of 1906. Finally, a land transaction was concluded in May 1927. Slightly over 11 acres of what had previously been the Menlo Park nursery of Michael Lynch along Oak Grove Avenue was deeded to the Dominican Nuns. Workers began to clear the property and contractors commenced erecting a group of buildings creating a Gothic monastery with an outer chapel, later acclaimed for its "elegant simplicity."

Nuns were brought from San Francisco, April 9, 1928. The new Monastery of Perpetual Adoration at Menlo Park, was dedicated with religious pomp and ceremony and a solemn Mass by San Francisco Archbishop Edward J. Hanna, August 5, 1928. Reminiscent of medieval European monasteries, this complex had magnificent stained-glass windows. It housed cloistered Dominican Nuns of the Corpus Christi, originally from New York, who had been temporarily quartered in San Francisco. By definition, cloistered nuns separate themselves from the world. At Menlo Park, sisters may leave for medical visits, to vote or occasionally meet elderly family members.

This group of Dominican nuns moved from temporary quarters in San Francisco to the new monastery in 1928.

BEHIND THE MONASTERY WALLS

Behind the walls of the monastery at Menlo Park, cloistered Dominican nuns, with modification, live a traditional religious existence. At its fullest, the monastery houses 50 nuns; by the end of the 1990s, the number had declined to 21.

While a few rise for personal prayer as early as 3 a.m., the community doesn't meet together until 5:30 a.m. Throughout their regulated day, nuns gather together six times for prayer. Designated hours are reserved for study, household work and recreation.

There are extensive gardens where sisters still work the fields raising their own vegetables and fruits. One piece of monastery equipment is a tractor. Until the 1960s when the practice ended, they raised their own chickens and milk cows.

Though television isn't forbidden, nuns have little time to watch. Sisters make all of their own clothing. For years, they baked altar bread hosts for distribution to Catholic churches throughout the Bay Area. During World War II, the breads were also baked for use by chaplains in the armed services. In recent years, when this task became overwhelming, altar breads have been baked elsewhere but distributed from Corpus Christi Monastery.

Sisters are distinguished for their work illuminating and translating books, most of which find their way onto shelves of colleges and universities. Some sisters, praised for their artistic abilities, create stationery and art works for sale.

Many aspects of their living haven't changed for centuries. However, the order has modernized in some ways. Sisters use automated voice mail. Most drive and may use the monastery automobile if required. A number are expert with computers. Monastery literature advises interested parties to "visit our web site."

Part of the monastery's equipment is a tractor. Nuns farm on 11 acres. Pictured is Sister Maria Christine.

DOMINICAN NUNS OF CORPUS CHRISTI

The clubhouse of the Italian-American Social Club was constructed in 1929.

ITALIAN-AMERICAN SOCIAL CLUB

AMEDEO AND RITA GADO

Amedeo Gado, one of the club's charter members, photographed in 1999.

The Italian population of Menlo Park became sufficiently large in 1929 that 32 men met to form the Italian-American Social Club. They constructed a rustic, one-story building on Oak Lane with a large meeting room and a bar. A free-standing kitchen was added later.

In the latter years of the twentieth century, the clubhouse, once far from the bustle of the town, is virtually in the heart of the business district just two blocks from busy Santa Cruz Avenue. The club is a place where friends meet to eat, drink, talk, and play boccie ball. "It gives us a chance to retain old traditions and our Italian heritage," states Amedeo Gado, one of the organization's charter members. Historically, Sunday nights, after children were in bed, folks gathered to drink wine and sing. "If Italians don't sing, they aren't happy," concludes Amedeo's wife, Rita.

As late as the 1990s, between 60 and 75 Italian men, most born on the Peninsula, gather for dinner on the first Tuesday of each month. Several times a year, wives and families join in. Beginning with the original dinners during the 1930s, the club provided members glasses only. At dinners, a "bring your own plate" rule has always applied.

Members regard annual picnics and traditional boccie ball tournaments as almost compulsory convocations.

AMEDEO AND RITA GADO

Traditional boccie ball remains the primary athletic pastime of the organization.

The Menlo Park Recorder was located on El Camino Real.

FROM THE MENLO PARK RECORDER, 1930

Town population in 1930 was 2,414.

The Milky Way Creamery, on Santa Cruz Avenue near the post office, touted as the finest such establishment on the Peninsula, sold ice cream cones for a nickel.

Mrs. P. Kelley, in search of a comfortable abode for her family, advertised that she was hoping to buy a four-room house. But she noted that she had no intention of paying more than $2,000 for such a place.

Meanwhile, Wall Meat Market sold fryers and broiling chickens at 37 cents a pound, leg of lamb was 39 cents, and lean sliced bacon was 35 cents a pound.

Menlo Park's Piggly Wiggly Store offered five pounds of potatoes for just 18 cents, 10 pounds of Sperry Flour for 45 cents, and four pounds of apples for 22 cents. A dozen jumbo eggs could be picked up for 43 cents and large loaves of bread were a dime each.

Gasoline in 1930 was 31 cents a gallon.

One of the town's better-known eateries, the Alabama Chicken Shack, was suddenly offering customers more than just food. Proprietors opened a miniature golf course adjacent to the restaurant. Some claimed that the course was surely "one of the most attractive recreation spots on the Peninsula."

Residents expressed a certain amount of glee over gasoline prices. By summertime, the price of a gallon was 31 cents.

Allied Arts Guild has been a Peninsula landmark since 1929.

ECHO OF HISPANIC CALIFORNIA

Allied Arts, created in 1929, a crafts guild similar to those found in Europe at the time, was built on four acres at Arbor Road and Creek Drive. The founders were Garfield and Delight Merner. The guild represented the vanguard of the state's arts and crafts movement devoted to the appreciation and promotion of regional handicrafts. Today, more than a dozen creative people from hat and tapestry makers to floral designers make and sell their products amid what appear to be old adobe and tile-bedecked gardens.

Mediterranean-style buildings were erected by the Merners in 1929. Gardens were designed by famed landscape architect Gardner Dailey. Paths were paved with stones from nearby San Francisquito Creek. Unique methods of handworking concrete were designed to simulate authentic tile floors and adobe brick. Wide swaths of cement between the arcaded walkways were gorged to simulate ancient wagon wheel tracks. Tiles and artifacts brought from Spain, Tunis and Morocco decorated the walls along meandering paths.

In 1932, the Merners invited the Palo Alto Auxiliary of what later became the Lucile Salter Packard Children's Hospital at Stanford to operate a lunchroom for their benefit at Allied Arts. Volunteers began a lunch-and-tearoom. In that there were no kitchens, they prepared food in private homes. The cost for a lunch was 75 cents.

The Merners retired in 1935. The Allied Arts Guild Associates bought the property in 1946. Five years later, ownership of the guild passed to the hospital's Woodside-Atherton Auxiliary.

PEDRO DE LEMOS

No light in the cultural history of Menlo Park shines more brightly than that of immensely talented artist and craftsman Pedro J. de Lemos (1882-1954). Nevada-born, he moved to Palo Alto in 1917 to become the first director of the Stanford Museum and Art Gallery. Many of his "California decorative" style pastel pieces were published in Stanford publications of the 1920s.

Lemos, with architect Gardner Dailey in 1929, designed the buildings for Allied Arts. They decided to maintain the original 1885 barn and surround it with Spanish Colonial structures. Murals and frescoes for which Allied Arts was to become renowned were inspired by Lemos. He contributed significantly to garden design, including the fountains and meandering pathways.

Although now largely forgotten, Lemos was a craftsman who did it all. He designed and built structures, was celebrated for wondrously detailed tile and iron grille works, was the founder of the California Society of Printmakers and wrote numerous books.

Lemos epitomized the American Arts and Crafts movement. Allied Arts Guild is perhaps his best memorial.

Unique styling of Allied Arts was much to the credit of Pedro de Lemos.

PHYLLIS MUNSEY

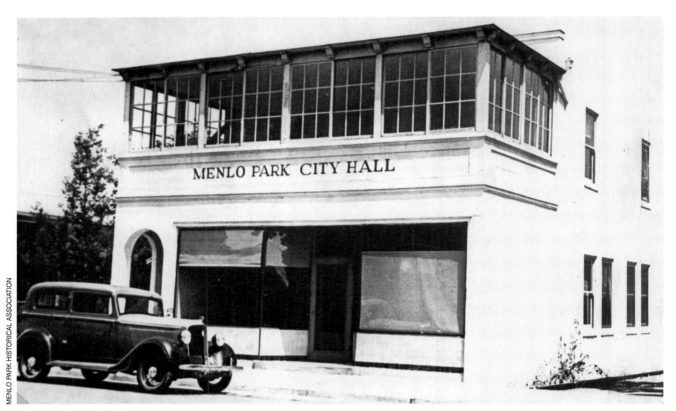

This building at 1036 Doyle Street housed all city offices for a decade.

ORIGINAL GOVERNMENT CENTER

Those who remember Menlo Park's first city hall at 1036 Doyle Street between Santa Cruz and Menlo avenues describe it as having been little more than a storefront. The desk inside the door belonged to the city clerk. Tables down the middle of the room served as the meeting place for the town council. Book shelves along the sides of the room comprised the public library. A partition across the back of the building, behind a locked door, was the police department.

By 1930, the police department consisted of the chief and two officers. Their only piece of equipment was an Indian motorcycle used primarily to control traffic along El Camino Real. The following year, a Model-A Ford (with rumble seat) was acquired for the department.

An elegant bus bearing the name, "The City of Menlo Park," was cause for public celebration.

A BUS TO BE PROUD OF

In 1938, the Pacific Greyhound Bus Line Depot and the Depot Cafe moved to new quarters at 1181 El Camino Real between Oak Grove and Santa Cruz avenues.

Company officials thought Ellen Hoss, the local agent, was doing such a fine job they wanted to repay her by christening one of Greyhound's fine new super-coaches "City of Menlo Park."

The decision became front-page news. In Menlo Park, Boy Scouts with circulars were sent door-to-door delivering personal invitations to the christening. Amid tremendous civic excitement at the Central Grammar School on July 31, 1938, the proud Hoss smashed a bottle of champagne across the prow of the glittering blue and silver bus. Townsfolk beamed seeing the name, "City of Menlo Park," inscribed across the front of the beautiful super-coach to travel the highways between El Paso and Portland and east to Salt Lake City.

Pacific Greyhound spent over $500,000 developing and testing this new generation of bus. The bus cost $20,000. Among other significant features, the "City of Menlo Park" was the first "air-conditioned" bus in America put into service by Pacific Greyhound.

Town Mayor James E. Cooper accepted the bus with an impressive speech. He declared that Pacific Greyhound had played a key role in developing Menlo Park by bringing thousands of people through town every year.

Bayshore Highway between South San Francisco and San Mateo opened in 1929. Menlo Park was reached in 1931. The highway became known for its bloody accidents.

BREAKING THE TRAFFIC BOTTLENECK

A modern roadway along the Peninsula was long overdue. El Camino Real, the County Road, was taxed beyond endurance. It was the busiest stretch of highway in the state.

"The bottleneck is broken," declared newspapers in September 1924 when San Francisco and Peninsula leaders met near South San Francisco to turn the first spadeful of dirt on Bayshore Highway.

The so-called "super highway" moved forward with agonizing slowness. San Mateo was not reached until October 20, 1929.

Bayshore's baptism in traffic came less than a week later, when one of the largest football crowds ever to assemble on the Peninsula headed for Palo Alto to watch the Stanford Indians battle the University of Southern California Trojans. At least 80,000 cars passed along the Peninsula that day. The Bayshore stretch, San Francisco to San Mateo, moved without delay. But from there, traffic was routed via Third Avenue to El Camino Real to complete the trip south. By mid-morning the old road had become a tangled snarl. The flow came to a virtual standstill and inched to Palo Alto. Some fans made it in three hours. Thousands missed the kickoff; a few never got there at all.

Bayshore, between Redwood City and Menlo Park, opened May 15, 1931, and was extended to Palo Alto the following year. Road workers didn't manage to complete the highway to San Jose until 1937.

*James L.
Flood*

JAMES L. FLOOD WAS FAMILY'S BLACK SHEEP

Silver king James C. Flood thirsted for respectability and acceptance by Menlo Park high society. That was why son James L. Flood (1857-1926), a notorious man-about-town, was such a disappointment. James L. became infatuated with beautiful Marie Rosina Fritz, later described by his annoyed father as a "woman of the Tenderloin."

The senior Flood offered Miss Fritz, an actress with the Victoria Loftus British Blondes Troupe Burlesquers, $25,000 to disappear. Although she tried, her distraught suitor followed; they were married in Italy in 1887. They returned to San Francisco but the new Mrs. Flood was never received by her husband's parents.

Exiled from the family, the couple lived in a 14-room flat at Page and Shrader streets. The largest room was set aside as the nursery for their daughter, Constance May. The child's mother died suddenly in 1895. Four years later, Flood married *her* vivacious younger sister, Maud Lee Fritz of Kansas City. Maud Lee apparently wasn't interested in raising her sister's child. Constance May was enrolled in a Roman Catholic convent in Kansas City. Nuns catered to her needs.

Maud Lee, the second Mrs. James L. Flood, as she appeared with her stepdaughter Constance May. The photo was snapped shortly after she married her dead sister's husband.

Flood provided for the girl's care but never saw his daughter again. Attempts by Constance to contact him were thwarted. James L. Flood and his new wife became parents of three children. It must be assumed none was told of the half-sister in Kansas City. Apparently, when Flood lay dying years later, he believed that Constance May had been successfully lost.

Constance May Gavin and her husband seated in court at Redwood City.

Judge George H. Buck

PATERNITY SUIT BLEMISHES FLOOD FAMILY NAME

James L. Flood died February 15, 1926. In addition to large amounts of real estate, his fortune was valued at approximately $20 million to be divided between his wife, a daughter and a son. (A second son had died in infancy.) Sharing also was Flood's never-married sister Cora Jane (Jennie) Flood.

But a bombshell convulsed the Flood family in August 1926, when a young woman, Constance May, filed in Superior Court asking for a daughter's share of the estate. A courtroom battle began in 1931 after years of pre-trial testimony. It was held in the Redwood City court of Judge George H. Buck.

Constance testified that she was the daughter of Flood. A mass of evidence was presented on her behalf. Family friends identified her. In all, 33 witnesses testified for her. On the stand, Maud Lee Flood adamantly denied the story.

The trial ended with dramatic suddenness. Though proceedings weren't yet concluded in August 1931, Flood attorneys petitioned the court to find in favor of the family. Buck obediently turned to the jury and read from a document handed him by the attorney. Was James L. Flood the father of Constance? The jury was instructed to answer "no."

Spectators were outraged. Sheriffs deputies cleared the courtroom. Ten of twelve jurors refused to sign the verdict.

Nevertheless, Constance May was legally disowned and disavowed. Under the law she was not Flood's daughter.

Residents of the Peninsula were invited to view the Flood estate when it was dismantled. Pictured is Dorothy Taylor Fallon at the entry to the great house.

DOROTHY FALLON

AGREEMENT WITH WOMAN CLAIMING TO BE FLOOD'S DAUGHTER

"Not a particle of evidence introduced in this case shows that James L. Flood was the father of the petitioner herein," declared Superior Court Judge George Buck when denying Constance May's bid for a new trial. But the California Supreme Court found that Buck had erred in directing a verdict.

Flood attorneys feared a rematch. On March 1, 1934, compromise was reached with the petitioner. The young woman was awarded approximately a million dollars.

Four weeks after the agreement, to pay legal expenses and provide for the award, the Floods announced that *Linden Towers* would be dismantled and the furnishings sold at auction. A number of rooms, including paneling and furniture, were sold to Hollywood film studios. The subdivided property became the Lindenwood district.

David D. Bohannon

BUILDER OF HOMES AND INDUSTRY

Not surprisingly, housing starts were almost non-existent during the Depression of the 1930s. Few builders considered it a good time to begin new suburban developments. But San Francisco-born contractor David D. Bohannon, an ambitious builder who during an almost half-century career was responsible for more than 40,000 homes, accepted the challenge to provide affordable houses.

He began building Belle Haven, a 540-acre residential subdivision on a flat plain in east Menlo Park adjacent to the marshes of San Francisco Bay. Ultimately the development included 1,305 units for people of low to moderate income. It was the only such project undertaken in the United States during the height of the Depression. Modestly priced single family houses, apartments, and duplexes were nestled among harmonizing shrubs and lawn.

Casa del Flores, a three-bedroom, Spanish-styled model home, complete with electric dishwasher and detached two-car garage, opened February 25, 1933. House lots averaged 50 feet in width and were 100 feet deep. Bohannon put affordable Belle Haven houses on the market beginning at $5,950.

During the early 1950s, the builder contributed to the further development of Menlo Park through the construction of the 200-acre Bohannon Industrial Park, a forerunner of Silicon Valley, located on the west side of the freeway. This enterprise included the construction of 96 buildings on 88 different lots.

Bohannon was the builder of the only Depression housing development in the United States.

San Mateo County Parks and Recreation Department

Of all county projects during the Depression, few were as successful as Flood Park.

FLOOD PARK IS LEGACY OF THE NEW DEAL

Flood Park is a San Mateo County-run regional facility located within the incorporated limits of Menlo Park. It is on Bay Road, west of Highway 101, between Marsh and Willow roads. The 23-acre park is known for magnificent oak and bay trees.

During the 1930s, San Mateo County purchased the property from descendants of silver millionaire James C. Flood. Park construction was undertaken in 1937 as a Works Progress Administration (WPA) New Deal relief project. The project provided 100 men employment for a year. Workers began by hand excavating for a large community swimming pool.

Buildings, still in use today, were constructed with adobe (dirt, clay and straw) made at the site. Bricks were molded using earth from the pool excavation and mixed with a secondhand bread-mixing machine acquired from a nearby bakery.

Structures required the manufacture of between 2,500 and 3,000 adobe bricks. Construction followed the ranch style made popular by architect Cliff May and featured in *Sunset Magazine.*

The park's headquarters building and restrooms were assembled with hand-sawed and hand-hewn redwood doors and beams cut by WPA workers in the redwood groves of San Mateo County's Memorial Park west of La Honda.

During the late 1980s, the once rustic park underwent a complete face lift to accommodate the almost quarter million people who used it annually.

Menlo Park's mayor James E. Cooper introduced Senator Samuel Shortridge at the dedication of Fremont Park (1938).

FREMONT MEMORIAL PARK

November 11, 1938. Former President Herbert Hoover came to Menlo Park to join U.S. Senator Samuel Shortridge in dedicating Camp Fremont Memorial Park at the corner of Santa Cruz Avenue and University Drive. Standing in the heart of the former camp where thousands of soldiers had been trained for the Great War, Hoover warned that the "forces of brutality and might are rising again" and summoned his listeners to be prepared to "again defend our independence and our honor."

Shortridge encapsulated the story of Camp Fremont, concluding: "I have the honor to dedicate this site to Fremont Camp comrades, to the end that it may be guarded, beautified, and kept as a memorial to all who served their country in the great war."

Festivities were climaxed by a colorful parade of Peninsula veterans. Menlo Park residents who were not members of the parade stood along Santa Cruz Avenue to watch. Following the festivities, a barbecue lunch for guests and participants was served at Kuck's Picnic Grounds at Oak Grove Avenue and Merrill Street.

Landscaping of the park was undertaken in 1940 by Menlo Park landscaper Albert Wilson. The Army arranged for permanent display of a three-inch saluting gun, a five-inch gun with breechblock and several trench mortars to "add to the beauty of the park."

Former President Herbert Hoover also participated in the dedication of the new town park.

MODERN TIMES COME TO EL CAMINO REAL

Menlo Park resident Joe McLoughlin vividly recalls wood sidewalks and a narrow, two-lane El Camino Real during the 1930s. The highway was "a high-class gravel road." But modern times were coming. McLoughlin reminisced about the young daredevil who raced through town one night at 40 mph, an unheard of rate of speed, even on "the highway." Big changes began in 1937. That's when the State of California undertook preparation to widen El Camino Real to transform it into a four-lane highway. Along the west side of the road, many of the buildings were raised and moved back between 30 and 50 feet. Other structures, not worthy of the effort, were destroyed and reconstructed.

The old Menlo Theater, later called the Guild, proved too substantial to be moved and was considered too important to be destroyed. Known for its spacious lobby, workers simply sliced half of it away to allow for the widened highway.

By spring of 1940, residents were already lamenting the changes. In March, three new service stations were to be added along the highway. "Menlo Park was once known as a village of beautiful oaks. It can claim that distinction no longer, rather it will be known as the town of hideous gas stations." In mid-July, it was reported that "only three corners in town are not occupied by oil stations and they may be purchased soon."

Modern times arrived in Menlo Park in 1937 with the widening of El Camino Real, transforming it from a country road into a major highway. Menlo Park Hardware at the corner of Santa Cruz Avenue was cut in half and moved to the west.

By the spring of 1940, the "town of beautiful oaks" had become the "town of hideous gas stations."

This ornate bedroom set sold to Universal Studios for $900.

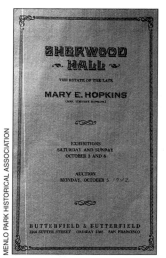

Butterfield & Butterfield auctioned hundreds of items. Many pieces had come to Hopkins from the days of Milton Latham.

SHERWOOD HALL DISMANTLED

Timothy Hopkins died in 1936. His widow followed him in death five years later. Fifty-room *Sherwood Hall* was bequeathed to Stanford University. Subsequently, officials ordered it destroyed to make way for construction of a World War II Army hospital.

Furnishings were to be sold. An auction, conducted by Butterfield & Butterfield of San Francisco, was held October 5, 1942. All of the 740 auctioneer's lots were purchased. Of 2,000 people who roamed the majestic rooms of *Sherwood Hall*, 200 became buyers. Each bedroom had its own marble-topped lavatory. Bathrooms were furnished with plush armchair commodes and huge marble tubs. It was a furniture lover's paradise. There were bedroom suites in walnut, mahogany, maple, ebony and other rare woods, all painted in intricate designs and inlaid with contrasting woods or mother of pearl. Connoisseurs ogled divans of a bygone era; chairs with tapestry seats and backs; lighting fixtures of Venetian glass and bronze; exquisite paintings; carpets and drapes beyond description. There were carved panels and doors of beautifully matched woods.

Hollywood movie studios were the most enthusiastic buyers. The highest price for a single item was $900 paid by Universal Studios for an ornate bedroom set. Warner Brothers acquired two bedrooms, one for $400 and the other for $500. The auction of antique treasures realized $20,000. Because of building material shortages created by the war, Universal Studios purchased, dismantled and trucked much of the actual structure.

Lt. Col. T.W.E. (Tom) Christmas, executive officer of Dibble Hospital, posed with area engineer Capt. Miner and secretary Jeanne Ward (Bone).

SPRAWLING ARMY HOSPITAL AT MENLO PARK

Jeanne Ward Bone was the first of Dibble General Hospital's 700 civilian employees when it was built in 1943.

The military hospital, named for Colonel John Dibble, one of the first high ranking Army Medical Corps officers to die during World War II, was a 94-unit, 127-acre complex designed for 1,726 patients. There were 64 buildings and miles of corridors located along Middlefield Road on the former Timothy Hopkins estate. Dibble's purpose was to relieve crowded conditions at Letterman General Hospital in San Francisco.

This objective changed in 1944 when Dibble was designated a center for plastic surgery to reconstruct battle-shattered and broken bodies. Blinded soldiers and those who had contracted eye diseases were also sent to Menlo Park. Reconstructions were painful and slow. One patient required 21 operations. Medical success became routine. Almost 2,600 patients were restored to "near normalcy."

By 1946, the facility had acquired a venerable air. Landscaping had taken root with 1,400 trees and 2,000 shrubs donated by local residents. There were great expanses of lawn. Though many hoped that Dibble Hospital would become permanent, it was ordered closed in 1946. For Jeanne Bone, the decision was disappointing: "It was the end of something special, we helped so many." She drove her car one last time around the deserted ground, admits to having had a good cry and throwing the hospital keys into the dust.

The Administration Building of Dibble General Hospital was typical military construction of the era.

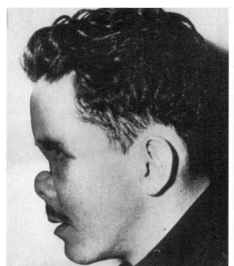

Plastic surgeons at Dibble Hospital rebuilt battle-scarred faces.

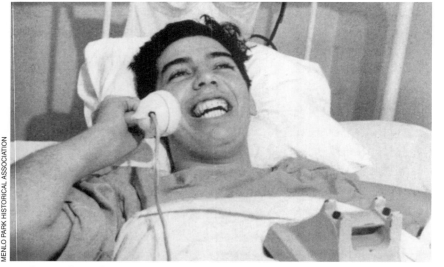

At the Menlo Park hospital, medical miracles became routine.

DIBBLE HOSPITAL'S AMAZING SERVICE

The hospital was dedicated March 2, 1944, a few days after the arrival of the first convoy of patients who had suffered injuries fighting in the Pacific. Before war's end, 16,268 wounded were given treatment in specialized fields of medicine.

Dibble was one of two hospitals in the nation that specialized in a rehabilitation program for the blinded as well as surgery and treatment for eye injuries in general. "We were limited in what we could do to help patients in the field hospitals," states Dr. Bernard Silber, "but at Dibble we all had the sense that we were doing everything we could to help...."

Incoming wounded included an extraordinary number of blinded soldiers. The hospital became a center for corneal transplant operations. Additionally, its role in the production, training and research in connection with plastic artificial eyes became a model used by other hospitals throughout the nation. Of 269 totally blind soldiers, 57 were discharged with near-normal vision. The less fortunate received plastic eyes.

The manufacture of a new, more nearly perfect form of plastic artificial eye was accomplished under the pioneering direction of developer Dr. Stanley Erpf. By June of 1945, approximately 5,100 such plastic prostheses had been made and fitted.

Improvements in reconstructive surgery techniques were pioneered at Dibble. Under Captain Walter D. Macomber, in charge of plastics, Dibble was the first hospital in the nation to perform surgery on burn victims and was among the pioneering institutions to make extensive use of pedicle, whereby tubes of flesh taken from victims' legs were used to grow skin back on sunken faces.

The Edward W. Hopkins house became Vallombrosa Center. *This picture was taken in 1908.*

(125) VALLOMBROSA CENTER

Vallombrosa, a grand home at 250 Oak Grove Avenue was the residence of Edward Whiting Hopkins (1860-1925), nephew of transcontinental railroad builder Mark Hopkins. The structure dated from the 1860s.

Hopkins, president of the Union Ice Company, was a director of Bank of California and the treasurer of Southern Pacific. He called his estate *Vallombrosa*, meaning "Shady Valley." The area reminded him of Tuscany, the Italian province whose capital is Florence. Hopkins imported trees from all over the world and planned extraordinary parties both inside and in the gardens.

In 1947, the central 10 acres of property and the house were purchased by the Catholic Church. *Vallombrosa* became the Bay Area's only retreat facility for women. Since 1947, three orders of nuns have conducted retreats at *Vallombrosa*. In current times, the center has been run by the laity and retreats are conducted for both men and women.

Other than the exquisite gardens, little is left of the old estate. The wood house has been covered with stucco. Large bedrooms on the top floor were renovated to accommodate 30 retreat participants; thin walls were erected to create private cubicles. Bathrooms complete with marble washstands are shared. Once luxurious parlors have been converted into rooms for meditation and reading.

Hanna Boys Center, an experiment of the Roman Catholic Church, began in Menlo Park.

HANNA BOYS CENTER

The Edward J. Hanna Center for Boys, an experiment of the San Francisco Archdiocese as a shelter for homeless and wayward youngsters between the ages of 11 and 14, opened a "demonstration unit" in several buildings on the southwest corner of Middle Avenue and Arbor Road in January 1945. Two buildings covered a third of the grounds, one housed the dormitory and the other, the kitchen and dining room facilities. A third structure was a workshop where the boys learned to work with machine and hand tools.

The facility was under the direction of a priest who worked with a staff of five.

This center, named for the late Archbishop Edward Hanna, was dedicated by then Archbishop John J. Mitty. "Prevention of delinquency is far less costly than correction," he stated. The center was started to gauge the need for establishing a permanent sanctuary for unwanted and neglected youngsters.

The Menlo Park facility, under the direction of a priest, had a staff of five. It served confused, insecure youngsters. The attempt was to create a setting where individual attention could be given to each boy. Boys attended local schools. "If all the school kids were as well behaved as those who came from the Hanna Boys Center," declared the local police chief in 1946, "there wouldn't be much to do."

Church authorities deemed the experiment successful. Twenty-four boys were accommodated initially; within a year, there was a waiting list of over 200. Menlo Park was too small for existing needs. But as a result of the experiment, a new Hanna Center was built on 170 acres in Sonoma Valley.

Little House, *as the name implies, was a humble enterprise when it opened in 1947.*

LITTLE HOUSE

In 1947, Dr. Russell Lee of the Palo Alto Medical Clinic called upon women of the Peninsula to do something creative about the community's growing numbers of active senior citizens.

Referring to themselves as the Peninsula Volunteers, the ladies, on April 1, 1949, opened *Little House*, a senior citizens center in a residence on Menlo Avenue. Originally with 12 members, the organization offered craft classes and provided a meeting place for people over the age of 50. *Little House*, so named because of the tiny cottage in which it was located, soon outgrew the humble structure. Peninsula Volunteers raised $80,000 for the construction of a spacious new building, which was erected at 800 Middle Avenue. That opened amid much celebration in 1954. A letter of congratulations was received from President Dwight D. Eisenhower.

In 1995, Jewish philanthropists Mervyn and Roslyn Morris provided for a million-dollar renovation of the entire facility. The building, owned by the City of Menlo Park, is leased for a nominal fee by Peninsula Volunteers. The organization continued to fund *Little House* through a variety of activities.

Mrs. Hall, director of Little House, *still ran a small operation in the early 1950s.*

On the occasion of its fiftieth anniversary in 1999, the center was lauded as one of the oldest active senior facilities in the nation. Today it boasts several thousand members. The facility includes a computer laboratory, community college classes, lectures, movies, craft classes and a full variety of senior citizen-centered classes.

Richard Laine is pictured in the chemistry laboratory of SRI International (1981).

SRI INTERNATIONAL

An influx of patients expected to flood Dibble General Hospital in 1945 never materialized. The government ordered the facility closed in October 1946.

The following year, newly-created Stanford Research Institute (since 1970 known as SRI International) moved into the former military buildings. For more than half a century, they served as SRI's campus. Scientists blazed trails and left indelible imprints in the lives of people internationally. Their innovations are felt daily and include everything from improved dish-washing detergents and oven cleaners to banking innovations and weaponry. During the 1950s, the nonprofit institute analyzed the feasibility of an amusement park for Walt Disney. Disneyland was ultimately built. Scientists there developed the computer mouse and later were instrumental in creation of the Internet. Magnetic ink used on account numbers on the bottom of checks, allowing electronic processing, was an innovation pioneered at SRI. The Institute also played a key role in the creation of stealth technology used on U.S. military aircraft, making them invisible to radar.

Students demonstrated against the Institute during and after 1969, protesting its involvement in weapons development. These protests led to a separation between the university and the institute and ultimately to a change of name.

Former President Hoover as he appeared in retirement at home on the Stanford campus.

GUIDING SPIRIT BEHIND SRI

Stanford's most illustrious alumnus, a member of the first graduating class in 1895, was square-faced Herbert C. Hoover (1874-1964). Hoover was a classic American success story, in every sense a true Horatio Alger. Iowa-born, he was orphaned at age nine. He worked his way through Stanford, finishing with a degree in geology and mining engineering.

It seems clear that there would have been no Stanford Research Institute without the encouragement, advice and wholehearted support of this man of vision. One of Hoover's long-range goals was the stimulation of greater productivity in American industry. He became a proponent of creating a scientific research organization aimed at developing new products, processes and techniques. He was convinced that a research institute would attract more people and more business to the Peninsula; land values would rise significantly.

Creation of the institute was long delayed by Hoover's election to the presidency in 1928, the Depression and World War II. The worldwide crises made it virtually impossible to find support for such a facility; the idea was placed in limbo. Nevertheless, it was Hoover's continuing interest and support which brought about the creation of SRI in 1946.

Until his death, Hoover played a significant role in the life of the Peninsula. During his presidency, the Summer White House was his home on the Stanford campus.

Herbert Hoover became the force behind creation of Stanford Research Institute.

The headquarters of Sunset Magazine, *designed by architect Cliff May, when it opened in Menlo Park.*

⑬⓪ # SUNSET MAGAZINE

Governor Edmund G. Brown was in Menlo Park November 17, 1964, for the dedication of a new $835,000 headquarters for *Sunset Magazine*. There was a flock of telegrams from governors and civic officials from seven Western states.

The 22,000-square foot Willow-North building, a streamlined single-story, rambling ranch style adobe with a redwood shake roof located at Middlefield and Willow roads, was designed by Western architect Cliff May of San Diego. The seven-acre, oak-studded garden was the work of landscape architect Thomas Church. Two additional buildings and a 4,500-bottle wine cellar were added later.

The headquarters gradually became a Menlo Park tourist attraction. Visitors, including many foreign dignitaries, regularly took 45-minute tours, the highlights of which were the gardens and test kitchens. The number of guests annually averaged 50,000. The gardens represented the flora of the whole Pacific coast.

Sunset, originally a San Francisco publication established in 1898 by the Southern Pacific to promote Western tourism, industry and agriculture, was named to honor the railroad's *Sunset Limited*, a luxurious passenger service between New Orleans and Los Angeles.

The company was purchased in 1928 by Laurence W. Lane Sr. for $65,000. Its first issue, representing a new concept in magazines, appeared in February 1929. Thereafter, *Sunset* became an enduring cultural institution as the "magazine of Western Living." It emphasized building, gardening, travel and cooking. At its height, circulation was 1.5 million. In 1951, when the company sought to leave San Francisco, Lane's sons, Bill and Mel, both Stanford graduates, convinced their father to move to Menlo Park. After the death of their father, Bill and Mel Lane assumed control of the enterprises: *Sunset Magazine*, *Sunset Books* and *Sunset Films*.

Employees of Sunset *were photographed on a coffee break in the building's interior patio in October 1951.*

The Lane family posed at the Sunset *headquarters. Left to right are Mel, Ruth Bell, Laurence and Bill. The family continues to be among Menlo Park's most philanthropic.*

PRINCIPLES GUIDED MEL AND BILL LANE

Sunset Magazine was a Lane family enterprise. During the 1930s, Laurence W. Lane's two sons, Mel and Bill (both of whom presently maintain offices at 3000 Sand Hill Road) hawked magazine subscriptions door-to-door. Their home economist mother, Ruth Bell Lane, assisted editing the magazine while writing a reader recipe feature.

Mel and Bill took over the *Sunset* operation in the 1950s. They were determined that the publication remain a lifestyle magazine for wives *and* husbands. It was not to become a women's magazine. Research showed that increasing numbers of men were interested in both gardening and cooking.

Results of this research also prompted the Lanes to continue their father's prohibition on advertisements for feminine hygiene products, only because such ads had a tendency to discourage male readers. The pair added liquor and tobacco to the type of ads they chose not to print. Wine was still acceptable in that it was part of the Western ethic, featured in cooking and was a "beverage of restraint." The Lanes also refused to advertise the National Rifle Association because theirs was a family magazine.

In 1969, when DDT was proven environmentally harmful, *Sunset* readers were warned against using products containing the chemical. Thereafter, the magazine refused to accept advertising from a major manufacturer of garden products, previously a primary advertiser, because of the company's continued use of the chemical.

Sunset was sold by the Lane family in 1990 to *Time Warner* for $225 million.

EARL DOUGLASS JR.

This 1953 graduation from Menlo School was held on the lawn of the former Leon Douglass estate, then the campus of the institution.

EVER-EVOLVING CHARACTER OF MENLO SCHOOL FOR BOYS

The character of the William Warren School changed with the retirement of its headmaster in 1923. Under new leadership and to the delight of students, the military nature of the institution ceased. It became the Menlo School for Boys.

But in 1927, upon the recommendation of Stanford University President Ray Lyman Wilbur, the school created a private tuition-supported junior college program. The first college classes were begun in the fall of that year. The name of the institution was changed to the Menlo School and Junior College, Ltd.

Menlo School offered classes for students in grades seven through ten. The junior college curriculum included the last two years of high school and the freshman and sophomore years of college. The two schools existed together for 22 years.

In the spring of 1946, the board of trustees of Menlo School was able to acquire the 55-acre Leon Douglass estate for use as a campus. The ornate house became the school's main building. The property was subdivided to generate money to pay for the transaction. Temporary metal buildings were moved onto the property for additional classroom and dormitory space. Trustees, in 1949, added the School of Business Administration and offered students the possibility of obtaining Bachelor degrees. The corporate title of the institution became Menlo School and Menlo College. They presently operate as separate entities.

EARL DOUGLASS JR.

Palatial Douglass Hall provided the setting for Menlo School's student lounge in 1969.

The day of all-male institutions was waning by the 1970s. In 1979, trustees voted to make the schools coeducational.

Brothers Bill and Dom Ryan proudly display their stock in 1929.

MENLO PARK HARDWARE

It was June 15, 1924, that Menlo Park Hardware opened to customers. Founder J. William Ryan (1894-1967) was also the first treasurer of incorporated Menlo Park. This bustling store at the corner of Santa Cruz Avenue (facing El Camino Real) catered to building and farming needs of the community.

Business expanded rapidly. In 1928, Ryan invited younger brother Dom (1907-1989), previously a cowboy and professional hunter, to become a partner. Dominic worked with his brother and later ran the firm, staying for 61 years. During the early period of town growth, he dealt with contractors determining hardware needs. He bid on jobs, giving estimates for the number of screens, hooks, hinges and screws that a contractor would require.

The store's stock changed significantly. During the first decade, there were iceboxes; then came refrigerators. There was the era of washboards; then came the more modern wringer washing machines. Piped gas became available in Menlo Park during the 1920s. The store sold and installed as many as 30 new stoves a month.

Menlo Park Hardware was one of the first businesses to move from El Camino Real to a new location at 700 Santa Cruz Avenue. As late as the 1990s, when the hardware store was run by a second generation of Ryans, kerosene lamps, stove polish, nails in bulk and even washboards were still stocked. But some items gradually disappeared from the shelves. There was no longer call for barbed wire, ammunition, dynamite, or cattle feed.

Dom Ryan was photographed in 1969.

This structure served as Menlo Park's second city hall. It later became the British Bankers Club.

CITY HALL

City Hall quarters were exceedingly cramped during the period after incorporation of the town. All municipal offices were located in a rented store on Doyle Street.

Finally, in 1939, Mayor James E. Cooper arranged for larger facilities, renting the bank building at the corner of Santa Cruz Avenue and El Camino Real. The elegant structure had been erected to house the Menlo Park Branch of the Palo Alto National Bank. (In later years, this was a branch of American Trust Company.) Like the original, this city hall was home for all city services.

That building was sold in 1948 just as the Army was announcing plans to abandon its hold on Dibble Hospital. Mayor Charles P. Burgess headed for Washington, D.C., to convince officials to allow the town to purchase a chunk of hospital property with the existing structures.

Successful in his quest, Burgess thus laid the foundation for what ultimately became Menlo Park's new civic center complex. Meanwhile, one hospital structure was used for city offices. Another became the council chambers. Though crowded and uncomfortable, these buildings served the town for 20 years.

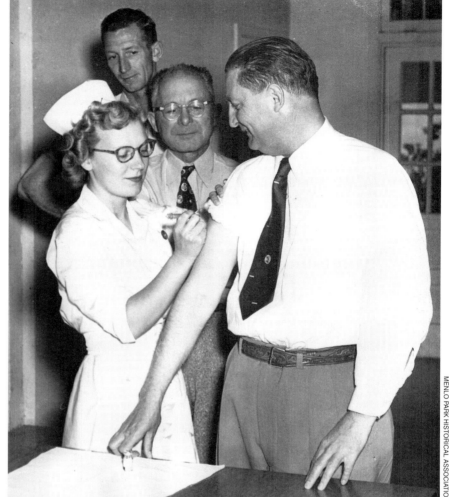

Mayor Charles Burgess received an inoculation against polio during the 1950s.

(135) # TOWN'S MASTERMIND

Alabama-born Charles P. Burgess (1905-1957) became one of California's best-known, small city leaders during the 1950s. A 1928 graduate of Stanford, he was elected to the Menlo town council in 1942 when the population was 3,000. He was mayor during 1945-1953 and again 1954-1955, when he also served as president of the League of California Cities.

Burgess brought about revolutionary changes in town after World War II. Though a daily commuter to San Francisco, he revitalized Menlo Park's downtown, then a shabby collection of buildings along both sides of El Camino Real.

While the California trend was toward development of suburban shopping centers, Burgess widened and improved Santa Cruz Avenue. Old houses between El Camino and University Drive were replaced by new businesses. Off-street parking facilities were created behind buildings on both sides of Santa Cruz.

In 1948, Burgess arranged for the purchase of a portion of the former military hospital property earmarking it for a civic center. Acquired with the purchase were park lands, a swimming pool, theater and gymnasium. Dilapidated barracks became city offices. The park was named for him.

Burgess was disturbed that the community had no high school and that students were bussed to Sequoia High School in Redwood City. Determined that Menlo Park should have a school of its own, Burgess ran successfully for a seat on the high school board. His goal was fulfilled when Menlo-Atherton High School was dedicated September 16, 1951.

Charles P. Burgess

Graduates of Menlo-Atherton High School remember the main hall. School clothes were significantly different during the 1950s.

MENLO-ATHERTON HIGH SCHOOL

A dedication to truth, liberty and tolerance was solemnly read by Robert J. Dell'Ergo, president of the Sequoia Union High School District board of trustees in his address to faculty, parents and friends, who gathered September 16, 1951 for ceremonies opening the long-awaited and now almost completed $1.5 million high school in Atherton. Dell'Ergo described the overcrowding of Sequoia High School and praised the people, notably Menlo Park Mayor Charles P. Burgess, also a member of the Sequoia board, who had led the fight to obtain this new school plant. Voters in 1949 provided for additional high school facilities authorizing construction of Menlo Park-Atherton High School. A proposed campus along Middlefield Road in Atherton was chosen and, in May 1949, the district purchased *Holm Grove*, the former Joseph A. Donohoe estate. A rambling single-story high school, often referred to as "the country club" because of its splendid location, was to serve students of Atherton, East Palo Alto, Menlo Park, Portola Valley and Woodside.

Although construction was still several months from completion, classes accommodating a student body of approximately 1,000 ethnically diverse students opened in fall 1951.

Students Shannon Stamps, Tashana Telser (Old Navy) and Emanuel Farrell relaxed at Menlo-Atherton High School in the year 2000. The school's symbol, the bear, is painted on the building opposite the administrative offices.

The Kavanaugh house, dating from 1906, became a well-known local landmark.

KAVANAUGH INDUSTRIAL PARK

During the 1950s, the Clarence Kavanaugh family still called their property east of the Bayshore "the field." For almost 100 years, the land in the Ravenswood district had been used for growing wheat and alfalfa. The family house, dating from the 1850s, was still in use.

On this property, located along Willow Road, Clarence Kavanaugh (1930-1993), great-grandson of Menlo Park pioneer Charles Kavanaugh, began the construction in 1955, of the 100-acre Kavanaugh Industrial Park, turning, as he said, "barley into buildings."

Within five years, the park had been completely leased. One of the first tenants contributing to the success of the project was *Sunset Magazine*. Twenty thousand feet of space was leased for the distribution and mailing of the periodical. In subsequent years, as circulation grew, *Sunset* footage increased. Other early tenants included Hiller Aircraft and Signal Oil Company.

Land on which the industrial park was erected had been acquired by Irish-born Charles Kavanaugh (1828-1900), one of Menlo Park's pioneers. He bought his first 150 acres in 1854. These were planted in wheat. The same property, for which he paid but a few pennies per acre, was soon valued at $1,000 per acre.

Moses Kavanaugh (second from left) is pictured with friends in 1930.

L. MACCHELLO

Few remaining examples of the ethnic strains which created local upheaval during the 1950s can still be found in Menlo Park. In the process of tearing down an old building in July 1999, this sign was discovered. It reads:

*Attention White People
This is the center [of the] colored section of town.
I will finance any colored... [de]siring to locate in Menlo Park.*
    *W.H. Guernsey
    Licensed Real
    Estate Broker
    444 California Ave.
    Mayfield*

BELLE HAVEN

Belle Haven, east of the Bayshore Freeway, was a 1930s housing development for the white working class. In the 1950s, when industry began to expand in that area, however, large numbers of African Americans sought homes in the neighborhood.

The "invasion" of Blacks caused alarm. This, connected with unscrupulous tactics by real estate companies, led to panic selling and an exodus by white residents. Belle Haven prices plummeted. A few homes reportedly sold for as little as $5. Within a few years, Belle Haven had become predominantly black.

Many new arrivals, especially those directly from the South, harbored resentment of police authority. Black residents who ventured onto the west side of the freeway commonly were detained for questioning. To most African Americans, embarrassed and humiliated by these tactics, the police became the "enemy."

Policemen, sheriffs, and firefighters responding to calls into Belle Haven were sometimes assaulted. Later, wearing of flak jackets for their personal safety became standard.

By the 1970s, in an attempt to defuse a potentially explosive situation, the city council set out to change the police image by portraying officers as less authoritarian. Blue uniforms, badges, pistols and billy clubs, all disappeared, replaced with slacks and ivy league blazers. Patrol cars were repainted pastel green and white.

L. MACCHELLO

During the 1980s, though still politically potent, the neighborhood's African American majority began to decline and Belle Haven became increasingly multi-ethnic. Significant numbers of Latin Americans and Pacific Islanders began moving in. Ultimately, by the year 2000, the Hispanic population had become the most dominant group. Houses in this section of town, which originally sold for under $6,000 during the 1930s, were bringing as much as $375,000 by the end of the century.

Young Terrence Hallinan was removed (1949) from a remote location in Yosemite National Park by a Hiller helicopter.

TOWN'S ROLE IN HELICOPTER HISTORY

Stanley Hiller Jr. moved his helicopter construction company to 1350 Willow Road in unincorporated Menlo Park in April 1948. He was one of the five largest helicopter manufacturers in the nation. The 61-acre site with highway and rail access near the Dumbarton Bridge was subsequently annexed to the city. Surroundings were flat enough to permit light airplane operations.

A near-disaster gave impetus to company growth. On July 31, 1949, 12-year old Terrence Hallinan, son of a San Mateo attorney, was thrown from a horse in an inaccessible area of Yosemite National Park, 8,100 feet above sea level. The boy suffered a skull fracture. Navy efforts to rescue him failed as did an attempt by the Bell Helicopter Company. Finally, at dawn on August 5, Jay Demming, Stan Hiller's chief test pilot, weathered sporadic winds and vicious air currents over jagged 10,000-foot peaks to pluck young Hallinan from his remote location and deliver him to safety.

This "almost-miracle" proved the worth of helicopters and had a major effect on company sales. There was an immediate surge of orders. A Yosemite ranger declared that the rescue, the first in the park's history, "opened a new era in removing injured persons from remote mountain areas."

At approximately the same time as this rescue, two other Hiller machines sold to the French for use evacuating combat wounded from remote battlefield locations in France's war to retain Indochina. As such, Hiller helped reshape the configuration of the late twentieth-century battlefield.

Prince Bernhard of the Netherlands (left) consulted with Stanley Hiller in his mission to acquire helicopters.

The aristocratic game of polo, played for years at the Menlo Circus Club field, always attracted crowds.

THE SPORT OF KINGS

Athletic types gathered in 1915 to form the Menlo Polo Club. For a decade and a half, before activities were suspended with the onset of the Depression of the 1930s, members, who leased the Menlo Circus Club field, gathered weekly to engage in this scientific and exacting game. Uniformly clad in high-heeled boots, white breeches, green and yellow shirts, white gloves and protective helmets, members relished the sport for its "elegant and exotic appeal." Often termed "the sport of kings," polo was a serious enterprise, far too solemn to be classed as merely a game. By 1893, the sport was played in California and the fashionable elite of the Peninsula took to it with relish.

Each practitioner was required to have a "string" of ponies. A player with fewer than six was looked upon as a rank amateur. When a match was in another town, horses were chauffeured about in luxurious private rail cars, many of which were more sumptuous than the most palatial Pullman cars.

It was a sad day when Menlo polo was suspended. But in 1954, San Francisco steel executive (and Atherton resident) William Gilmore, an avid practitioner of the sport, revived the Menlo enterprise. Under his direction, the grass at the Circus Club was finally cut and the Polo Club's lease renegotiated.

Thereafter, polo on the Circus field has been played twice a week.

William Gilmore (right) talks with polo great Eric Pedley. Gilmore was responsible for returning the "sport of kings" to the Menlo Circus field.

Architect Kingsford Jones designed the new Menlo Park civic center. A time capsule was buried in 1974 (three stepping stones from the flagpole) between the council chambers and the administration building.

CIVIC CENTER FULFILLS LONG-TERM DREAM

Following acquisition of one-time Dibble Hospital property in 1948, two decades of planning and development by the city and architect Kingsford Jones went into the creation of Menlo Park's first true civic center.

City Library, a one-story $120,000 structure approved by voters in 1956, opened along Ravenswood Avenue the following year, becoming the first component of the new center. A $246,000 police station, the second component of the center, was approved by voters in 1960. This gave the department 10,000 square feet of offices. The basement contained a shooting range and armory.

Until 1963, city-sponsored recreation programs had been centered in the Dibble Hospital gymnasium. That year voters approved a $450,000 bond for a 15,000-square foot recreation center to be located on Mielke Drive near Alma Street. This was the third component of the civic center project. Other recreation facilities were maintained, including the Dibble gymnasium, a swimming pool and baseball diamond, all located in Burgess Park, across Mielke Drive.

The final component of the civic center was the city hall, including the council chambers, completed in 1970.

No Peninsula civic center compares with Menlo Park's. Pictured is the lake (yet to be filled) with the administration building in the background.

JEWEL OF THE CIVIC CENTER COMPLEX

"Completion of this civic center marks the beginning of a new era for Menlo Park and its citizens," declared Mayor Ira E. Bonde at its dedication, October 18, 1970. Others affirmed that the center was a symbol that the town had "come of age."

A just-finished spacious and comfortable, million-dollar city hall now housed seven departments of town government. Tinted glass windows made it possible for employees to gaze out on fountains and a lake in front of the building.

Margaret Snowden, who served as city clerk for almost 30 years, was delighted with the new building, noting that employees had once worked elbow-to-elbow in a tiny cramped office: "They now have room to breathe in three times more space."

A feature of the building was the mayor's office suite. A single desk was placed in the redwood-paneled private office where either the mayor or any individual council person could greet visitors. It was adjoined by a five-desk council office.

The center's focal point became the redwood and glass council chamber erected on the edge of a man-made lake a few steps from the administration building.

Within this square building, both audience seats and council table were placed at 45-degree angles relative to the walls to create an illusion that the high-ceilinged chamber was diamond-shaped.

Landscaping of civic center grounds combined existing ancient trees with carefully chosen new ones.

LANDSCAPING THE CIVIC CENTER

Even when the complex was completed in 1970, landscaping did not have the raw look of new planting. Grounds, planned over a 15-year period by noted Palo Alto landscape architect Arthur Cobbledick, had a residential flavor. Severe lines, characteristic of many public gardens, had been avoided.

Cobbledick molded the center's flatness into gradual slopes and sunken areas to add interest. Existing trees, among which were 12 live oaks, large elms, four *Sequoia Sempervirens* and five Chinese ginkgoes, were protected. Cobbledick added beds of flowering annuals for color.

For many, the most outstanding feature of the design was the artificial lake with 11,500 square feet of water surface. Cobbledick included rapids, a two-foot waterfall and a rustic wooden bridge. The lake was surrounded by moss and lichen-covered fieldstones. Water flowed through the lake at 400 gallons per minute, assuring a complete turnover every two-and-a-half hours.

Cobbledick augmented the existing vegetation with Japanese cherry trees, red-flowering chestnuts and dwarf pines. The design was highlighted by a free-standing fountain donated by *Sunset Magazine*.

The story of Menlo Park Public Library has been one of continual expansion and growth.

Dr. S. Wing Chan was one of the major supporters of the library and civic center.

MENLO PARK CITY LIBRARY

Voters approved a $5 million bond issue in 1989 for the expansion and renovation of the city's public library at 800 Alma Street. This intensive project began in 1991 and was completed in June the following year.

Added had been 7,677 square feet, bringing the total to 34,046. New stacks, with earthquake-resistant shelving, provided for a 40 percent expansion of the library's collection, which then comprised 127,000 books and video tapes.

This opening was the last step of a long journey that had begun March 9, 1916, when the San Mateo County Library opened a branch in Menlo Park's Central School on El Camino Real. Then, the book collection contained 50 titles. Townsfolk only had access to them, after school hours, for a single hour per day. During early years, the library was treated like an unwanted child. In 1926, it was moved to the vacant barbershop of the antiquated Kuck Hotel. Later, portions of two city halls on Doyle Street and at the bank building on El Camino Real were reserved for stacks.

Not until 1956, after the acquisition of hospital property, was a new library planned and erected. Though elegant, the 5,500-square foot Kingsford Jones-designed building was also soon inadequate. A 12,400-square foot addition was appended to it in 1968. Librarians seemed convinced that no further expansion would be necessary. That is, until the mid-1980s when approval for the $5 million bond issue was sought.

UNITED STATES GEOLOGICAL SURVEY

Following World War II, the U.S. Geological Survey moved to Menlo Park. It was drawn by the proximity of Stanford University and the offer of free government land (the former Dibble Hospital property).

For seven decades after its creation by Congress in 1879, scientists of the U.S. Geological Survey worked out of offices in Washington, D.C. But following World War II, it was decided that personnel should be stationed closer to where actual research was being accomplished. One office opened in Denver and a second was established in California.

Because of the closeness of Stanford University, Menlo Park was chosen as the Western Regional Center. The specific site, 16 acres of one-time Dibble General Hospital, was property once owned by Milton Latham and later Timothy Hopkins.

The Geological Survey took possession in 1954, occupying a number of the antiquated hospital buildings. Although new structures were erected and the old ones gradually disappeared, as late as the 1990s, six of the original buildings remained in use. One, a pinkish-brown, tar paper shack, thought to have been part of the Dibble Hospital pharmacy, received landmark status in 1994 but was demolished two years later.

At Menlo Park, there are presently 800 employed. In this academic environment, there are water quality laboratories and an Earth Science Library with a collection of approximately 300,000 volumes.

Survey scientists involve themselves with everything from volcanic and earthquake studies to the investigation of unique clams that have moved into San Francisco Bay.

A quarter of the work force is engaged in the study of earthquakes. There are highly sensitive seismographs continuously recording even the slightest ground movement occurring anywhere in the West.

These tar paper shacks were used as USGS laboratories until the last one was destroyed in 1996.

USGS geophysicist David Oppenheimer is shown checking aftershocks of the Loma Prieta earthquake of 1989.

GEOLOGICAL SURVEY'S UNIQUE ROLE

The Western Mapping Center opened as part of the U.S. Geological Survey in 1959. Its responsibility was to provide the fundamental work for the nation's map makers. During the Center's first quarter century of existence, 23,000 maps were drawn.

Not only was the Center responsible for creating data and standards for maps used in national defense but for maps sold in gas stations and used by the American Automobile Association. Hikers, surveyors and urban planners depend on the Center's famed topographic maps. All maps are available to the public.

Until the 1980s, while Americans had been successful in mapping the moon and analyzing the terrain of other planets, little was known about the nature of the ocean floor off the West Coast of the United States. During that decade, using a sensitive sonar device, marine geologists from Menlo Park put together the first "road map" of 250,000 square miles of ocean floor between the Canadian and Mexican borders.

Drawing topographical maps is a specialty of USGS. Pictured is Wayne Kobayashi at work in 1988.

Sharon Heights, once the exclusive realm of Frederick Sharon, overlooks Stanford University and the town of Menlo Park.

PLANNED COMMUNITY IN THE HILLS

In 1957, the 574-acre estate once owned by Frederick Sharon in the hills west of town was sold for subdivision. Developers Duncan McDonald and Mark Radin envisioned a residential community of half-acre homes, condominiums, town houses, churches and schools. Ultimately there would be businesses, a shopping center and a country club. Eleven acres were set aside for Sharon Park, bordering on an artificial lake.

The Sharon Heights Country Club was conceived of as a real estate sales incentive. Club membership during the 1960s could be purchased for $3,500. By the end of the 1990s, that cost had risen to $110,000.

Some residents who moved to Sharon Heights during its developmental years were still there at the end of the century. Most agree that the environment was unique and many also feel that the completed subdivision maintained much of this early appeal. There were still spectacular sweeping panoramas of the bay and surrounding hills.

Homes are located minutes from Stanford and are on the doorstep of Silicon Valley. Such an ideal location contributed to the dramatic rise in property value. Houses that sold originally for $50,000 now command between $900,000 and $1 million.

model
583 THE SHARON

GARAGE KITCHEN NOOK DINING
ACTIVITY RM LIVING RM
ENTRY BATH
BDRM HALL BATH
BDRM BDRM

A generously planned home thoughtfully designed for years of comfortable family living and entertaining.

Sharon Heights

From 1959 until 1963, the one-time "cottage" of Frederick Sharon doubled as the temporary Church of St. Denis. Services were conducted on the porch or in the ballroom.

REBIRTH OF ST. DENIS PARISH

St. Denis Catholic Church was reborn in 1959 when the San Francisco Archdiocese purchased 14 acres of land in Sharon Heights. Father Thomas I. Kennedy arrived at Menlo Park in June 1961 to become the first pastor of a new St. Denis Parish to be located at Avy Avenue and Monte Rosa Drive.

Accompanied by his dog "Rua," Kennedy moved into the former 32-room Frederick Sharon "cottage" overlooking all Sharon Heights. He recalls the gorgeous 14-foot ceilings and enormous 16-burner, three-oven stove "on which I cooked my one egg for breakfast."

Until completion of the new church, this historic home doubled as both parish and rectory. Kennedy was the only occupant, living in a small upstairs room. A parish office with telephone was on the first floor. Most rooms had fireplaces.

In July 1961, Kennedy celebrated the parish's first Mass for a dozen parishioners on the veranda of the house. When it rained, services were conducted in the ornate ballroom. There was no heat. This long-empty home soon became the scene of fund-raising activities, including a New Year's reception, barbecues and a costume ball.

Parishioners moved into their new church in June 1963.

Only the Gate Lodge Survives

The gate lodge at 555 Ravenswood Avenue, once part of the Barron-Latham-Hopkins estate, is one of Menlo Park's cherished surviving treasures of a bygone era. This structure was erected in 1864 for William E. Barron. In 1871, owner Milton S. Latham enlarged the building, adding a mansard roof. The estate's superintendent resided there.

Following 1906, although the big house, *Sherwood Hall*, did not sustain serious structural damage, gas lines leading to and throughout the building were ruptured by the earthquake. At that time, owner Timothy Hopkins vacated the main house, moving his wife and daughter into a redecorated and cozier gate lodge.

Stanford University acquired control of the estate in 1941. Even after the big house was dismantled and removed, the gate lodge remained. In 1968, Stanford officials sold the gate lodge along with 1.1 acres of land to the City of Menlo Park. The structure was renovated for use by a variety of different groups.

Today the gate lodge and mermen fountain are all that remain of the once palatial Sherwood Hall.

MENLO PARK HISTORICAL ASSOCIATION/KEN YIMM

The Menlo Park Post Office (c. 1890) was located on Santa Cruz Avenue near the railroad tracks. This was the quaint town so often remembered by Miss Gale.

SUSAN GALE PRESERVED TALES OF OLD MENLO

Her contribution to the town was unique. Susan Gale (1887-1969) appears to have been one of the first to recognize that the town had a colorful and important past. She has often been referred to as the "first lady of Menlo Park history." Gale gathered newspaper articles, brochures and scrapbooks of early families and artfully bound them together with stories of friends to preserve the history of the community.

Gale made history in her own right. In 1908, an era before many women went into business, she enrolled in Heald's Business College in San Francisco. Thereafter, she was employed in Menlo Park as a bookkeeper at Duff & Doyle's general store before beginning a 32-year banking career with the Bank of Palo Alto.

Gale approached the town's history as a participant. Many key events had been part of her life. She regarded residents lovingly, almost as if they had been her own family. But as a recorder of history, she was seldom able to distance herself from them. While claiming that she wanted to capture a true picture of early Menlo, her tales were filled with affection and nostalgia for a kinder place she had once known. Gale frequently uncovered "small unhappy indiscretions" and felt it was her responsibility to suppress them. Upon the celebration of Menlo Park's centennial in 1974, her efforts were applauded. One writer reported admiringly that such "indiscretions" died with her.

Miss Susan Gale, one of Menlo Park's best-loved personalities, delighted in telling tales of the town. She firmly believed that unpleasant indiscretions were best forgotten.

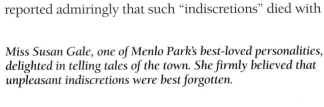

In 1969, students, angered by weapons development at Stanford Research Institute, demonstrated against the institution. This demonstration ultimately assumed riot proportions.

ANTI-WAR FURY EXPLODES

Anger directed against U.S. involvement in Southeast Asia during the 1960s and 1970s erupted in Menlo Park. This movement was spearheaded by Stanford English professor H. Bruce Franklin and College of San Mateo student-activist Aaron Manganiello. Their organization, "Venceramos" (Spanish for "We will win"), created in 1966, was openly Maoist and called for the overthrow of the United States government.

Identifying Venceramos as a "multi-national Communist organization," Manganiello initially called for unity of Blacks, Chicanos, Asians and Native Americans. Ultimately, he rallied all dissenters, regardless of race.

In Menlo Park, with the largest minority community of any city on the Peninsula, Venceramos' anger was directed against the Stanford Research Institute because of its defense contracts. Rioting erupted in Palo Alto in May 1969; the crowd was dispersed by helmeted police after helicopters sprayed the demonstrators with tear gas. One hundred demonstrators, many of whom were anti-war-minded students from Stanford, were arrested. Later in the day, demonstrators moved against SRI facilities in Menlo Park.

Harassment of city officials, "the bourgeois establishment," reached a peak in September 1971 when Venceramos turned out in force at a meeting of the city council. They stood on seats and ground cigarettes out in carpets. Police Chief Victor Cizanckas and other officials feared for their lives.

"The air was electric," declared City Manager Mike Bedwell. "There were enough police with shotguns behind the curtain that if anybody had made a wrong move, there could have been a lot of blood spilled."

Stanford Professor H. Bruce Franklin (pointing) led students in anti-war protests.

Police Chief Victor Cizanckas revolutionized the Menlo Park department.

MENLO PARK HISTORICAL ASSOCIATION

MENLO PARK HISTORICAL ASSOCIATION/JOE MELENA

Menlo Park police officers grew long hair and attempted to appear non-threatening. Pictured is Officer Larry Shannon.

INNOVATIVE TOP COP ALTERS POLICE DEPARTMENT

Victor Cizanckas, a six-year veteran of the Menlo Park Police Department, became chief in 1968. Within four years, his department became nationally recognized for innovative programs and its overall approach to crime. Assaults against police officers declined. By 1971, burglaries had declined by 35 percent; homicides, rapes, grand thefts and felonious assaults in the city had as well.

What was the difference? Cizanckas believed it was because his men no longer looked like cops. "I'm a firm believer in the principle that clothes maketh the man," declared the former U.S. Marine Corps officer turned cop. The 42-man force no longer wore paramilitary police uniforms. Instead, officers donned natty green blazers, ties and brown slacks. Black and white patrol cars were also replaced with pastel green and white ones.

Military ranking was abolished. Gone were the detective bureau, the traffic division and all motorcycle officers. Rules and procedures books that usually governed all aspects of a patrolman's job were tossed out.

Officers wedded to traditional police procedures were appalled; approximately half the department resigned. Cizanckas left in 1976. While many of his progressive changes were maintained, a new chief brought about a return to traditional blue police uniforms.

Billy Ray White was the first African American elected to the Menlo Park town council.

MAYOR BILLY RAY WHITE

White served three terms as mayor and is remembered for his direct approach and parliamentary skills.

Billy Ray White, a resident of Belle Haven and father of six, was just what Menlo Park needed during the racially volatile years of the 1970s and 1980s. He was more than just the first African-American mayor and the only Black ever to serve on the town council, when Billy Ray White spoke, everybody listened.

He had the support of the Chamber of Commerce and friends on both sides of Bayshore. After seven years on the planning commission, in 1978, he was elected to the town council. White served three terms as mayor (1980-1981, 1982-1983 and 1985-1986).

White is remembered warmly. He was blunt, direct and usually down to earth. He surfaced at a time when there was much angry talk from dissatisfied residents of Belle Haven and little was getting accomplished.

A strong voice for his Belle Haven neighbors, he was also an effective facilitator. Once he joined the council, good things began to happen. "He was full of energy and was wonderful," states journalist Marion Softky. David Wheaton, assistant city manager during the 1990s, speaks of White with admiration. His leadership in town didn't end when he left the council. "He connects with everybody and is still a powerful force in the community," concludes Wheaton. Former city manager Mike Bedwell states, "He has an excellent conceptual ability and can listen to both sides of a question...and finds a middle ground. He puts ideas together."

Born and educated in Texas, where he attended college at Prairie View A & M, White arrived in Menlo Park with his family in 1964. "We liked it here and just didn't bother to go back."

White's colleagues agree that dull meetings were enlivened with his sharp wit and healthy laugh. "He really knew how to run meetings," remarks longtime city clerk Margaret Snowden. "When he was in charge, I got home from council meetings early."

Tons of garbage were dumped east of town for the creation of a bay-front park.

Garbage became a bonanza for Menlo Park. Methane gas, generated from deep inside the garbage mound, produces electricity for 3,000 homes and brings $180,000 a year into the city coffers.

STINKING DUMP BECOMES MAJOR PARK

A 160-acre park, located at Marsh Road and Bayfront Expressway, had its beginning in 1957 as an abandoned salt pond. It became a county disposal dump. The property was given to the city on the condition that all profits go into a fund for the creation of a city park. Ultimately $7 million in dump fees were collected. Officials began planning the park by 1974. Rubbish was carefully sculpted to create the foundation for hills and meadows.

The last garbage was dumped in 1984. Gradually it was covered with clay and topsoil. The $4 million make over created hills, trails and unparalleled views of the San Francisco Bay. "Mount Trashmore," as the park's highest peak is commonly known, rises 80 feet above the bay's surface.

Bayfront Park opened in 1989 with 2.2 miles of perimeter trail, in addition to seven miles of bicycle paths and another eight miles of hiking trail. Grasses and trees had been planted; parking lots and a sprinkler system were added.

Continuously decaying garbage beneath the park, since 1984, has produced an ongoing supply of methane gas, an unexpected bonus for the city. The combustible methane is used to power turbines and generate electricity. Enough is drawn from the landfill to provide 3,000 homes with electricity annually. City revenues have been expanded by $180,000 a year.

The 3000 Sand Hill Road business complex is the most prestigious on the Peninsula.

LEGENDARY REAL ESTATE ENTREPRENEUR

Perhaps no person left a more indelible imprint on Menlo Park than real estate developer and philanthropist Thomas W. Ford (1921-1998). During the 1970s, he became one of the Peninsula's wealthiest businessmen.

Born in Ohio and a graduate of Yale with a law degree from the University of Michigan, Ford moved to Palo Alto in 1955. For a decade he served as legal counsel for the Stanford University Business Office and as Stanford's director of land development. In 1964, he created Ford Land Company, a real estate investment firm that developed and operated offices along the Peninsula. Ford was the driving force in making Sand Hill Road an epicenter of venture capitalism.

He recognized a need to accommodate emerging venture capital firms and wanted to create "the best office environment in the world." In this quest, Ford built the prestigious office complex at 3000 Sand Hill Road. This magnificently landscaped site, which opened in 1978, became a mecca for venture capitalists and in a very real sense was the heart of Silicon Valley. Rents there are 20 percent higher than those in midtown Manhattan.

By 1995, Ford Land Company owned 20 buildings and was the leading developer of the Sand Hill Road corridor. At the time of Ford's death, it was estimated that the approximately 40 firms along the corridor controlled as much as one-third of the nation's $12 billion in venture capital.

Tom Ford was also a most generous philanthropist. He was a major contributor to the Peninsula Open Space Trust and the Peninsula Community Foundation.

He once commented that he couldn't understand people who "didn't enjoy giving money away."

Thomas W. Ford

Since 1987, the Connoisseur's Market Place has become a much anticipated annual event.

CONNOISSEUR'S MARKET PLACE

The celebration began in 1987. Visitors to town on July 25 and July 26 found Santa Cruz Avenue closed from El Camino Real to Fremont Park. It had been transformed into a *Connoisseur's Market Place*, complete with covered garden dining pavilions, wandering musicians and window displays. There were over 250 exhibitors, craftsmen and artists. An amazing 90 percent of the town's merchants participated.

Sounds of guitars and flutes mixed with the tinkle of wind chimes. There were platforms for musicians. The Palo Alto Chamber Orchestra String Quartet provided music to shop and eat by. Local theater guilds performed.

The summer fair, touted as a quality event sponsored by the Chamber of Commerce, attracted almost 10,000 each day. People wandered the corridor sipping sparkling water, imported beers and white wines from black-stemmed commemorative glasses.

Attempting to protect Menlo Park's upscale image, backers of the fair announced that it catered to only the "the most discriminating connoisseur." Food booths offered gourmet selections ranging from crab ravioli and blue corn quesadillas to Cajun shrimp, oysters on the half shell and crepes.

The *Connoisseur's Market Place* has become an annual tradition.

BOOKSTORE AND LOCAL INSTITUTION

Roy Kepler (1920-1994) established a hole-in-the-wall bookstore on El Camino Real near the Guild Theater in 1955. He stocked 3,500 titles and was the first Peninsula bookseller to sell paperbacks.

When Kepler's opened, Eisenhower was president, the Korean War had just ended and U.S. Senator Joe McCarthy was conducting attacks against "the dastardly threat of an international Communist conspiracy."

Roy Kepler had been a World War II pacifist and founder of the War Resisters' League. His store was the Peninsula hub for anti-violence, anti-war and later anti-Vietnam movements. Revered by liberal-thinking people for his intellectual integrity, Kepler made his store a forum for controversial speakers, some known to be Communists. Albeit popular, Kepler's was viewed by many in the community as a hotbed of pacifism and "Commie Pinkos." Clark Kepler, Roy's son, who reluctantly took over store operation in 1988, recalled that, during early years, the family received death threats; rocks and hatchets were thrown through store windows. Once, a bomb was taped to the building.

In 1989, after several moves, a new 10,000-square foot store opened in the Menlo Center on the east side of El Camino Real at Ravenswood Avenue. Touting itself as "a store with book sense," with 112,000 titles, Kepler's is today the largest independently owned bookstore on the Peninsula.

Controversial Roy Kepler established the largest independent bookstore on the Peninsula.

Roy's son Clark took over active management of the bookstore in 1988. Here he supervises construction of the new 10,000-square foot store located at the corner of El Camino Real and Ravenswood.

Draeger's broke ground for a 13,000-square foot Menlo Park store in 1955.

CORNER GROCERY WITH CLASS

Perhaps no Menlo Park business is better known than Draeger's, a multi-million dollar food emporium which opened a 13,000-square foot store just a block off of Santa Cruz Avenue in 1955.

Draeger's looks for "a special kind of customer." That is someone who wants a broad selection of items and believes that quality is worth the price. The Draeger family determined that Menlo Park, sandwiched between Palo Alto and Atherton, while only a short hop from Portola Valley, was the ideal location to find such upscale customers. Today the store stocks $150 a bottle vinegars and $900 a bottle wines.

The present Draeger's, a 46,000-square foot food emporium, has both a gift shop and restaurant. It is one of the largest food stores on the Peninsula.

The Draeger's story has been one of continual expansion. In 1989, the store undertook a unique building project. A two-story market at 1010 University Drive was built around the existing single story building. The store remained open throughout the renovation. During summer, after the roof had been torn off, there was an unseasonal rain and customers were drenched. At least one simply put up an umbrella and continued shopping. Upon completion, the new store, including an upstairs restaurant and gift shop, constituted a 46,000-square foot expanse.

Until the end of the century, any food store with a 20,000 item inventory was considered large. The streamlined Menlo Park store maintains 60,000 items. There are 175 full-time employees.

Draeger's, now with three stores on the Peninsula, had its origins in San Francisco in 1925.

Police Officer Lisa Sims (1988) demonstrates the department's modern firepower.

POLICE GET MORE FIRE POWER

Our policemen "must never be outgunned," declared Chief Bruce Cummings in 1997. Officers had witnessed drive-by shootings in east Menlo Park. "I got to feeling that some of the people in our community were better armed than the police."

City Manager Jan Dolan concurred. Authorities began installing assault rifles in police cars to replace traditional shotguns. Cummings noted that such weapons fire more ammunition in less time. Both accuracy and range are greater.

Menlo Park police cars were soon equipped with submachine guns which held 32 rounds of ammunition. The new weapons could be fired one shot at a time, semi-automatically or fully automatically, a blast of 32 rounds in three seconds. Chief Cummings reported that Colt submachine guns took the place of old-fashioned, 12-gauge shotguns, which could fire only six shots before being reloaded. The shotguns were effective only at close range; with the new weapons officers could engage targets at 200 yards.

By the 1990s, Menlo Park police officers were also carrying semi-automatic pistols in their holsters.

The Menlo Park Police Department has become the best-equipped on the Peninsula.

*The Menlo Park Fire
Protection District, which
today serves Atherton, East
Palo Alto, and Menlo Park,
was authorized in 1918.*

MENLO PARK FIRE PROTECTION DISTRICT

*Fire district personnel
undergo special training
to make rescues in unique
situations. Pictured is the
hazardous materials team.*

In 1998, when the Menlo Park Fire Protection District posted three vacancies, 1,400 applications were received. The District, including Atherton and East Palo Alto, is one of the Peninsula's most prestigious and efficient. Its equipment is the most modern.

The district boasts, in addition to traditional fire-fighting tools, an air boat and several Kawasaki jet skis allowing firefighters to skim across the surface of the marsh to rescue boaters or wind surfers who run into difficulty.

Fire personnel also teach advanced rescue training to firefighters from across the nation. Graduates are equipped to shore up collapsed buildings, rescue people from tunnels and burrow through wreckage of buildings or freeways. Since 1989, approximately 1,000 firefighters have been taught to deal with such specialized rescue situations.

Training isn't all theory. Less than 24 hours after a bomb blast in an Oklahoma City Federal Building, April 20, 1989, a team from Menlo Park was airlifted to Oklahoma City. Members tackled the upper floors of the nine-story building, moving tons of concrete searching for survivors.

*Special district equipment
permits operations on the
bay marsh.*

During the course of a generation, Coach Parks acquired a reputation for academic prowess, coaching skill, evangelical spirit, and overall leadership at Menlo-Atherton High School.

COACH IS LEGEND IN OWN TIME

Ben Parks was hired to coach football at Menlo-Atherton High School in 1968. Says his friend Buzz Williams: "Parks is fair, consistent and tough. He is a fathering kind of coach who feels his kids are his responsibility for the rest of their lives."

"The Coach," as he has always been known, was born to a poor North Carolina family (1934) and came to Hollister in 1945. "I wasn't a great student," he admits. Parks attributes much of his success to Mrs. Florence Patterson, his teacher who made him repeat the sixth grade. "I hated her then but it worked," he adds with a hearty smile. "That was more than 50 years ago. Now she is a good friend. I visit her regularly."

He played football at College of the Pacific. "The famed Amos Alonzo Stagg was my kicking coach. He was 96 years old and had coached for 70 years." Following graduation, Parks himself began a coaching career at Stockton's Edison High School (1958-1968); simultaneously he was principal of Peterson Juvenile Hall.

Today, perhaps no other Menlo-Atherton faculty member is better known, more liked or held in greater regard. Parks was vice-principal, 1971-1972, head football coach, 1968-1984 and head wrestling coach, 1968-1999. Students, goaded on to greater deeds by the Coach's enthusiastic and inspirational briefings, regard him with admiration.

Besides traditional duties, Parks is a personal trainer for the San Francisco Forty-Niners. He has helped rehabilitate injured players, including Joe Montana, Ronnie Lott and Jerry Rice, working with them on weights, running, speed, endurance, flexibility and motivation. These legendary players became fixtures working out with Parks at Menlo-Atherton field.

A father of five and an ordained minister (in addition to being an educator), Parks feels an obligation toward the less fortunate in the community. For years he has personally provided food, clothing and even shelter to families in need.

Parks retired from coaching in 2000.

Coach Ben Parks

The Oasis Beer Garden on El Camino Real opened in a former Camp Fremont building. The front office of this structure was used as the air raid warden's office during World War II.

TOWN'S LEGENDARY OASIS BEER GARDEN

The noise level is always high. Customers shout to be heard. Patrons consume peanuts by basketsful and toss shells about on the floor. Students sing ribald songs and tell filthy jokes. They like the place, states one coed, "because it is always full of lowlifes."

Beer flows and the savory odor of pizza inundates the place. The best-selling meal is a greasy hamburger with fries. According to legend, it just may be the Peninsula's best burger.

This is the Oasis Beer Garden, a fixture on the west side of El Camino Real just north of San Francisquito Creek since Prohibition's repeal. Housed in an old Camp Fremont structure, a few claim that the Oasis is El Camino's oldest eating establishment.

Since it was established, the Oasis has been a popular student hangout. Bartender Pat Carrillo is pictured (1987).

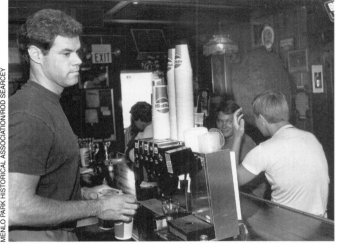

Attempting to explain its success, Oasis management points to bare light bulbs, messy floors and tables (walls and even ceilings) carved with initials of Stanford athletes. They say it is all "ambiance." One deeply carved round table hanging on the wall is said to have been in Charlie Meyers' Mayfield saloon. Managers proclaim that the Oasis "gets destroyed daily."

The long-standing reputation of the Oasis attracts a roster of famed patrons. Young John Fitzgerald Kennedy once dropped by to sample the hamburgers.

Regulars are faithful. One year, when the nearby creek flooded and water poured in, most Oasis customers took off their shoes and partied as usual.

Once humble Menlo Park Presbyterian has grown into the mega-church of the Peninsula.

Rev. Walt Gerber

TOWN SPAWNS A MEGA-CHURCH

For 70 years since it was established during the 1870s, Menlo Park Presbyterian Church was a sleeping giant. Its congregation was often almost non-existent. The awakening came in the years after World War II.

The original white steepled church on Santa Cruz Avenue was replaced with a Modified Gothic structure in 1951. Today it has become a mega-church and is recognized as one of the largest Presbyterian churches in the nation. There are 5,300 members; more than 9,000 attend regularly. On Christmas eve 1999, 12,000 attended services.

Five services are scheduled per weekend. Congregants arrive early if they want a seat. At peak times, hundreds crowd into overflow rooms to watch services on closed-circuit television. Just getting to church can be an ordeal. Cars line up for blocks. A half-mile walk from a parking space is usual. "The church property resembles a gridlocked shopping center at Christmas," states Pamela Fisher, wife of one of the ministers.

There are nine ordained ministers and a paid staff of almost 100. Included on the payroll are a media consultant and a full-time chef. Dinner is served once weekly for almost 500 parishioners. The church's annual budget is $6 million.

People come from as far away as Gilroy and every East Bay community. Senior Pastor Walt Gerber, evangelical in his approach, emphasizes the need to modernize and reach out to parishioners; 48 percent of the congregation is single. Three ministers on the staff are singles specialists. In spite of its widespread appeal, Gerber still sees this as a community church. Eighty-two percent of its members live within a 10-mile radius of the church; 46 percent live within three miles.

Suburban Park, one of many town neighborhoods, is known for its community spirit.

MENLO PARK DURING THE 1990S

Because of the town's geographic location in the southern part of San Mateo County and easy access to the community via the two major freeways, during the decade of the 1990s, the phenomenon known as Silicon Valley began converging on Menlo Park. Prices of real estate skyrocketed.

Nevertheless, the historic town, thanks in part to its many unique neighborhoods — Belle Haven, Felton Gables, Flood Triangle, Hillview, Linfield Oaks, Lorelei Manor, Sharon Heights, Suburban Park, West Menlo, Willows — has managed to maintain its identity and community personality.

This has always been a family town. By the end of the twentieth century, eight of the families who established Suburban Park in 1945 still had homes there. When developed, owners stipulated that these homes were to be made available only to former military personnel. Two-bedroom homes sold for $10,750 and three-bedrooms for a thousand dollars more. Fifty years later the same houses were selling for close to half a million dollars.

ENDURING DEPOT IS SYMBOL OF "ONCE UPON A TIME..."

It was a gala celebration, Independence Day, July 4, 1983, when Menlo Park Mayor Billy Ray White welcomed guests to the ceremony dedicating the 116-year-old Menlo Park Train Station as a historical landmark. Four years later, officials gathered again on the old station platform to mark completion of a thorough facelift and rededication of the depot as the town's Transportation Center.

That quaint structure, the oldest railroad station in San Mateo County and the town's most cherished historical relic, was again acclaimed as the focal point of downtown Menlo Park. With a newly landscaped, park-like setting, the antique depot tied together most of the downtown, including the civic and community centers.

Renovation had been funded by private donations and the California Department of Transportation. Dedication ceremonies were held in front of the CalTrain Station, following the 5:55 p.m. arrival of the southbound train. A parade was staged featuring old and new transportation modes, including classic cars and an antiquated fire truck.

Today no other surviving landmark so thoroughly symbolizes Menlo Park. The unique structure, built by the railroad across from the famed gateway erected by the town's earliest pioneers, has been silent witness to the community development — the colorful era of the grand estates, the growth of a tiny hamlet and its ultimate evolution into a dynamic city.

Menlo Park train depot, the Peninsula's oldest, is considered a treasure of the community.

MENLO PARK HISTORICAL ASSOCIATION

ACKNOWLEDGMENTS

The authors wish to acknowledge the following organizations for contributing photographs and information for use in this book:

Allied Arts Guild (Menlo Park)
Archdiocese of San Francisco
Atherton Heritage Association
Bancroft Library (Berkeley)
California Historical Society
California State Library (Sacramento)
City of Menlo Park
College of San Mateo
Corpus Christi Monastery
Hanna Boys Center (Sonoma)
Judah L. Magnes Museum
Menlo Circus Club
Menlo College
Menlo Park Historical Association
Menlo Park Presbyterian Church
Menlo Park Public Library
Menlo Polo Club
Menlo School

Palo Alto Historical Association
Peninsula Volunteers, Little House
Redwood City Public Library
Sacred Heart Schools
Saint Patrick's Seminary
San Francisco History Center, San Francisco Public Library
San Mateo County Historical Association
Stanford University

Many private families and individuals also made photographs and materials available to us, far too many to thank individually. Throughout the book, except in rare cases where donors have specifically asked not to be identified, photographs are credited to those who lent them. Photographs not otherwise credited are the property of the authors.

This has been a community project. Special credit is due to many agencies within the town of Menlo Park, including the Police and Fire departments, the City Clerk, the Planning Department and the City Manager's office.

The authors wish to single out several key individuals for special appreciation. Jeanne Thivierge, local history specialist for the Archives Committee at the Redwood City Public Library and Pat Akre, photograph librarian at the San Francisco History Center, San Francisco Public Library, spent many hours helping assemble the photographic essay of Menlo Park. Darwin Patnode, Ph.D., executive director of the San Mateo County Community College District Foundation, is acknowledged for his continuing advice and encouragement along with his assistance in preparing the final manuscript for publication. Jeffrey Burns, Ph.D., archivist for the San Francisco Archdiocese volunteered considerable effort helping us locate deeds and tie up loose ends. These individuals generously assisted the authors far in excess of normal expectations.

Photographs have been honestly reproduced. That is, they have not been electronically altered. The authors wish to extend their appreciation to Stephen Haag and the staff of Haag 'n Haag Photographic Services in San Mateo where many old and delicate original photographs were faithfully reproduced.

Finally, the authors acknowledge the hundreds of town residents, past and present, who have responded to requests for information or have come forth with valuable historical material.

DONORS

This book was made possible by the generous contributions of the following:

AARP Menlo Park #2545
City of Menlo Park
David D. Bohannon Organization
Draeger's Supermarkets Inc.
Ford Land Company
Gentry Magazine
Live Oak Lions
Mervyn L. Brenner
   Foundation, Inc.
Pacific Peninsula Architecture
Pacific Peninsula Group
Palo Alto Historical Association
Peninsula Building Materials Co.
Peninsula Community Foundation
Raychem Corporation
SRI International

Richard C. Angus
Mr. and Mrs. L.M. Anstead
Fanny H. Arnold
Dorothy and Fred Backlund
Louise J. Barbour
Lucille Barnett
Betty Beckers
Dan and John Beltramo
Lois Blackmarr
Mary and John Bohler
Jeanne W. Bone
William P. Brosge
Blanchard Buckhout
Elizabeth and Dick Buckley
Sarah L. Bush
Mr. and Mrs. Frank Carney
Jaye and George Carr
Rich Carter
Louise Cassell
Jeanne Chambers
Pat Clark
Mr. and Mrs. Edward Cleveland
Dorothy Shepard Cooper
Nancy Couperus
Olga Curusis
Leonore and Howard Daschbach
Niel and Nancy Davidson
Olga Devincenzi
Paul C. Diebels

William and Glendawyn Doyle
Mr. and Mrs. Douglas W. Dupen
George and Edith Durfey
Martha Eakland
Nancy Fenner
Arthur Flegel
Karen Fredrickson
Amedeo and Margherita Gado
Christine Gallinetti
Blanche Gardiner
Al Giannotti/Vela Corporation
Dr. Lorraine Godfrey
Liz Goldberg
Timothy Goode
John Goodwin
Mr. and Mrs. Gerald R. Grant
Mr. and Mrs. Colon C. Gulledge
William H. Harris
Harry and Barbara Hallett Harrison
Eugene Frank Helfrich
Rosemary C. Holding
Joan and John Inglis
John R. Johnson
John D. Jorgenson
Rev. Edwin Kennedy
Willis Knapp
Donald and Gay Kocmich
Eloise Lancestremere
Ambassador Laurence W. "Bill" and
   Mrs. Jean Lane
Marie R. Larabie
Barbara Mason
Duncan L. Matteson
James A. McFaul
Harriet McGinley
Bernie and Yvette McLoughlin
Joe and Eleanor McLoughlin
Ernst and Betty Meissner
Lauren Mercer
Carlos Merrick
Frank and Clarice Merrill
Mark Merrill
Frank A. Morris Sr.
Frederick J. Morris
Nancy Morrow
Helen and John H. Morse
Helen M. Musso

Barbara Norris
Mr. and Mrs. Robert Oakford
Ruth O'Shea
Mr. and Mrs. Louis Paponis
Claire Peterson
John Preyer
Mary C. Rauen
Elena Reese
Elizabeth K. Reinhart
Paul and Mary Ann Robbiano
Elizabeth Rovetto
Sally and Bill Russ
Grace M. Sain
Barbara J. Seaney
Mr. and Mrs. Roger Seccombe
Lawrence R. Simonini
Lorie and Sam Sinnott
Frank Small
Harold F. Smiley
Margaret E. Snowden
Nita Spangler
Robert J. Stephens
Ruth I. Stonehouse
Robin A. Sutton
Bill and Janet Tarr
Elton N. Thompson
Louise F. Triano
Phyllis Van De Mark
Jarmila Vrana
Adrian Ward
Clifford Walker
Denyse and Lyman Wear
Dr. Joseph B. Weeden
Bill and Jeanne Weseloh
Robert L. Whitney
Barbara Wood
Elinor Wood
Gil Workman

INDEX

A

Adams & Blinn, 32
Adams, Ansel, 32
Adams Banking & Express Company, 18
Adams, Cassandra Hills, 32
Adams, William James, 32, 44, 67
Adelante Villa, 55
African Americans, 154, 169, 177
Agassiz, Louis, 41
Alabama Chicken Shack, 125
Alemany, Joseph S., 37
Allied Arts Guild, 45, 126, 127
Allied Arts Guild Associates, 126
Almendral, 26, 84
American Theater, 77
American Trust Company, 150
Ancient Order of Hibernians, 9
Argonaut, 53
Argüello, José, 17
Argüello, José Ramon, 17
Argüello, Luís, 17
Argüello, Maria, 17
Arts & Crafts Movement, 127
Atherton (city), 10, 14, 41, 44, 117, 118, 120
Atherton, Faxon D., 7, 20, 21, 24, 54

Atherton, Faxon D. Jr., 26, 27
Atherton, Florence, 41
Atherton, George B., 52
Atherton, Gertrude, 37, 52, 53

B

Bank of California, 36, 60
Bank of Palo Alto, 166
Barron & Forbes, 28
Barron, William E., 28, 34, 165
Bayfront Park, 170
Bayshore Highway, 130
Bedwell, Mike, 167, 169
Belle Haven, 134, 154, 169
Belmont, 25
Beltramo, Alexander, 51, 94, 108
Beltramo, Billy, 81
Beltramo, Giovanni (John), 9, 51, 80, 108
Beltramo's, 51
Blake, Alfred E., 120
Bohannon, David D., 134
Bohannon Industrial Park, 134
Bonde, Ira E., 158
Bone, Jeanne Ward, 139
Borica, Diego de, 17
Bowie, Henry P., 96

Brady, Frank, 66
Bright Eagle, 61
British Bankers Club, 150
Broadman, George C., 44
Brown, Edmund G., 146
Buck, George H., 132, 133
Burgess, Charles P., 150, 151, 152
Burgess Park, 157
Burlingame Country Club, 84
Butterfield & Butterfield, 138
Byde A Whyle, 90

C

California Column, 40
California Society of Printmakers, 127
California Volunteer Infantry, 40
Camp Fremont, 13, 51, 61, 91, 98, 99, 100, 101, 103, 104, 105, 106, 107, 108, 109, 136, 178
Camp Fremont Base Hospital, 104, 105, 109
Carter, George, 68
Caruso, Enrico, 110
Cedro Cottage, 71
Central Grammar School, 74, 129, 160
Chamberlain, Selah, 114

Chan, S. Wing, 160
Charlie Meyer's Saloon, 94, 108, 178
Children's Circus of Menlo Park, 115
Chinatown, 75
Chinese, 8, 9, 59, 71, 74, 75, 160
Christmas, Thomas W.E., 139
Church of Nativity, 19, 42, 43, 62, 95
Church of the Nativity of the
   Holy Virgin, 67
Church, Thomas, 146
"City of Menlo Park" Bus, 129
Cizanckas, Victor, 167, 168
Clark, Warren D. (Mrs.), 86
Cobbledick, Arthur, 159
Coleman, James Valentine, 65
Coleman, Maria O'Brien, 64, 65
Comstock, 41, 48, 60
Connoisseur's Market Place, 172
Convent of the Sacred Heart, 12, 78, 95
Cooley, L.P., 44
Coon, Henry P., 54, 55
Cooper, James E., 129, 136, 150
Corpus Christi Monastery, 123
Coyote Point, 100
Crowe, Matthew, 11
Cummings, Bruce, 175

D
Dailey, Gardner, 126, 127
Dana, Richard Henry, 41
Dell'Ergo, Robert J., 152
Demming, Jay, 155
Dennis, Clifford, 97
Devlin, Charles, 78, 79
Dibble General Hospital, 14, 15, 138,
   139, 140, 144, 150, 151, 157, 160, 161
Dibble, John, 139
Disneyland, 144
Dolan, Jan, 175
Dominican Nuns of the
   Corpus Christi, 122, 123
Donahue, Peter, 42
Donohoe & Kelly, 36
Donohoe, Emilie Blain, 36, 88
Donohoe, Joseph A., 36, 88, 152
Donohoe, Joseph A. II, 36, 43
Donohoe, Mary Emilie
Douglass, Earl Jr., 111
Douglass Hall, 148
Douglass, Leon F., 80, 110, 111, 112
Douglass, Victoria Adams, 110
Doyle, James R., 66
Doyle, John T., 9, 18, 37, 44, 51, 62
Doyle, Murtha Joseph, 66
Doyle, R. Emmett, 18
Doyle, William A., 70
Draeger's, 174
Duff & Doyle's, 8, 9, 10, 66, 70, 76, 166
Duff, Michael, 66
Dumbarton Bridge (auto), 119
Dumbarton Bridge (railroad), 89
Dumbarton Point, 89

E
Edwards, Brent, 113
Ehrman, Ray, 97
Eisenhower, Dwight D., 143
El Camino Real, 8, 14, 137
Elkins, Marie Louise, 39
Elmwood, 33
Elwood, J. H., 57
Episcopal Parish of the Holy Trinity, 32,
   41, 67
Erpf, Stanley, 140
Eyre, Edward E., 40, 41, 67
Eyre, Edward L., 41
Eyre, Mary Tutt, 40, 67

F
Fair, James G., 48
Fair Oaks, 7, 10, 26
Fair Oaks (house), 31, 42
Fallon, Dorothy Taylor, 133
Farrell, Emanuel, 152
Felton, Charles Norton, 39, 44, 54, 67, 70
Felton Gables, 39, 73
Fennwood (See also *Petite Forêt*), 96, 114
Fisher, Pamela, 179
Fleishhacker, Herbert, 41, 77
Flood, Constance May (See Constance
   May Gavin)
Flood, Cora Jane "Jennie," 50, 132
Flood, James "Jimmy," 114
Flood, James C., 8, 41, 48, 49, 50, 63, 131
Flood, James L., 49, 131, 132, 133
Flood, Marie Rosina Fritz, 131
Flood, Mary Emma, 48
Flood, Maud Lee Fritz, 131, 132
Flood Park, 135
Flynn, Mary, 45
Foley, Mother Mary, 88
Ford Land Company, 171
Ford, Thomas W., 171
Franklin, H. Bruce, 167
Freeman, Harry C., 98
Fremont Memorial Park, 136
French Laundry, 113
Fretz & Ralston, 36
Furman, Dolores, 121
Furman, Thomas E., 121

G
Gado, Amedeo, 80, 124
Gado, Margherita "Rita" Ardizzoia, 80,
   112, 124
Gale, Susan, 166
Gansl, Alexander, 61
Gardener Nerve Sanitorium, 100
Gavin, Constance May, 131, 132, 133
Gerber, Walt, 179
Gilmore, William, 156
Girvin, Bob, 97

Glen-Eyre, 41, 77
Goñi, Dominga de (Atherton), 21, 53
Goodall, Charles, 72, 96
Goodall, Perkins & Company, 72
Grant, Frederick Dent "Buck," 50
Grant, Julia, 50
Grant, Ulysses S., 39, 50
Graves, William S., 106
Greenway, Ned., 86
Guild (Menlo Theater), 137

H
Hahn, Albert, 72, 96
Hahn, Harriet Rose Fenn, 96, 114
Hahn, Louise, 114
Hallinan, Terrence, 155
Hanna Boys Center, 142
Hanna, Edward J., 122, 142
Harbo, Charles, 11
Harrison, Benjamin, 10, 39, 73
Harron, H.P., 54
Hayes, Rutherford, 13, 39
Hays, Charles M., 72
Hearst, George, 39
Heart's Ease, 29
Heller, Clara Hellman, 90, 91
Heller, Emanuel S., 90
Hiller Aircraft, 153, 155
Hiller, Stanley, Jr., 155
Hoitt, Ira D., 11, 12, 77
Holbrook, Charles, 33
Holbrook, Merrill & Stetson, 33
Holbrook, Olive (Palmer), 33
Holm Grove, 36, 43, 93, 152
Holmes, Oliver Wendell, 41
Holy Cross Cemetery, 62, 63
Hoover, Herbert, 136, 145
Hopkins, Edward W., 67, 77, 86, 141
Hopkins, Frances Sherwood, 86
Hopkins, Mark, 59, 86
Hopkins, Mary Frances Sherwood, 59
Hopkins, Mary "May," 59, 138
Hopkins, Timothy, 10, 59, 73, 77, 138,
   139, 161, 165
Hoss, Ellen, 129
Hostess House, 101

I
Incorporation, 6, 14, 44, 118, 120
Internet, 144
Irishmen, 8, 45
Italian-American Social Club, 124
Italians, 9, 80, 124

J
Jenkins, Oliver Peebles, 71
Johnson, George C., 24, 29, 116
Johnson, Kate, 29, 79
Johnson, Robert C., 29
Jones, Kingsford, 157, 160
Jordan, David Starr, 56, 69, 94, 95

K

Kavanaugh, Charles, 153
Kavanaugh, Clarence, 153
Kavanaugh Industrial Park, 153
Kavanaugh, Moses, 153
Kelham, George, 83
Kennedy, John Fitzgerald, 178
Kennedy, Thomas I., 164
Kepler's Bookstore, 173
Kepler, Clark, 173
Kepler, Roy, 173
Kesey, Ken, 109
Kimball, Tappy, 88
Knight, Samuel, 77
Kobayashi, Wayne, 162
Kuck, Diedrich, 38
Kuck, Martin, 11, 38, 70
Kuck's Picnic Grounds, 136

L

Laine, Richard, 144
Lancestremere, Eloise, 68, 75, 113
Lancestremere, Laurent, 113
Lane, Laurence W. Sr., 146, 147
Lane, Laurence W. Jr. "Bill," 146, 147
Lane, Mel, 146, 147
Lane, Ruth Bell, 147
La Robleda, 90
Larrecou, Marie, 113
Larrecou, Pierre, 113
Latham, Milton S., 7, 28, 34, 35, 54,
    138, 161, 165
Lathrop, Ariel, 71
Laurel Court Hotel, 61
Laver, Augustus, 64
Lee, Russell, 143
Lemos, Pedro J. de, 127
Leonardi, Ursula, 75
Letterman General Hospital, 139
Linden Towers, 8, 49, 63, 64, 76
Lindenwood, 49, 133
Little House, 143
London & San Francisco Bank, 34
Loomis, George, 67
Lucile Salter Parkard
    Children's Hospital, 126
Lynch, Michael, 10, 63, 122

M

MacBain, John, 68, 74, 76, 77
Mackay, John W., 48
Macomber, Walter D., 140
Macondray, Atherton, 62
Manganiello, Aaron, 167
Maple Manor, 92
"Marco Polo," 88
Marie Antoinette Inn, 61
Martin, Dennis, 19, 43
Marvin, Charles, 71
Masonic Hall, 120
May, Cliff, 135, 146
Mayfield Grange, 46

McBean, Peter, 114
McDonald, Duncan, 163
McGlynn, Daniel C., 6, 116
McLaren, John, 90, 104
McLoughlin, Joe, 137
McNear, Frederick, 77
McNutt, Maxwell, 55, 114
Menlo-Atherton High School, 36, 151,
    152, 177
Menlo Circus Club, 114, 115, 156
Menlo Country Club, 84
Menlo Park, 8, 24, 32, 63, 143, 165
Menlo Park City Hall, 128, 150, 157, 158
Menlo Park Civic Center, 157, 158
Menlo Park Fire Protection District, 176
Menlo Park Gateway, 6, 113, 116
Menlo Park Hardware, 6, 137, 149
Menlo Park Historical Association, 6
Menlo Park Hotel, 11, 38, 160
Menlo Park Improvement Club, 11
Menlo Park Nursery, 63
Menlo Park Police Department, 121, 128,
    157, 167, 168, 175
Menlo Park Post Office, 166
Menlo Park Presbyterian Church, 54, 57,
    58, 76, 179
Menlo Park Public Library, 128, 157, 160
Menlo Park Railroad Station, 6, 25, 56, 181
Menlo Park Recorder, 125
Menlo Park Villa Association, 8, 24
Menlo Polo Club, 156
Menlo School & Junior
    College, Ltd., 148
Menlo School & Menlo College, 148
Menlo School For Boys, 97, 148
Merner, Delight, 45, 126
Merner, Garfield, 45, 126
Merrill, Leslie, 25
Mesdames of the Sacred Heart, 12, 88
Meyer, Charlie, 94
Meyer, T. Lemmon, 61
Mezes, Simon M., 24
Milky Way Creamery, 125
Miller & Lux Company, 92
Miller, Henry, 92
Miller, Nellie Sarah, 92
Mills, Darius Ogden, 60
Mills, Edgar, 60, 61
Mitty, John J., 142
Mixed American & Mexican
    Claims Commission, 37
Monastery of Perpetual Adoration, 122
Morris, Mervyn, 143
Morris, Roslyn, 143
Mount Trashmore, 170
Murphy, Eugene, 86
Murray, John, 45
Musso, Helen, 113

N

Native Daughters of the Golden West, 100
Native Sons of the Golden West, 116
New York Mining Exchange, 34
Nickel, J. Leroy, 92
Noel, Emma, 61
North Pacific Coast Railroad, 34
Nuthall, Carmelita Parrott, 65

O

Oak Grove Villa Hotel, 68, 76
Oakmeadows, 90
Oasis Beer Garden, 51, 94, 178
O'Brien, William, 41, 48, 64, 65, 87
Ockley, 92
Ohlone Indians, 16
O'Keefe's Saloon, 108
Oklahoma City Federal Building, 176
Oliver, Dennis J., 6, 24, 29, 116
One Flew Over The Cuckoo's Nest, 109
Oppenheimer, David, 162

P

Pacific Coast Military Academy, 61
Pacific Greyhound Bus Line, 129
Pacific Mail Steamship Company, 30, 45
Palace Hotel, 82, 83
Palmer, Silas H., 33
Palo Alto (city), 10, 12, 120
Palo Alto (house & estate), 46, 47, 77
Palo Alto (tree), 16
Palo Alto Auxiliary, 126
Palo Alto Medical Clinic, 143
Panama-Pacific International
    Exposition, 96
Park, Royal W., 61
Parks, Ben, 177
Parrott, John II, 36
Parrott, Noelie Christina, 36, 43
Payne, Pauline O'Brien, 87, 110
Payne, Theodore Fryatt, 87
Pedley, Eric, 156
Peninsula Hotel, 100
Peninsula School, 65
Peninsula Volunteers, 143
Permanent Court of Arbitration at
    The Hague, 37
Petite Forêt, 72, 96
Phelps, Timothy Guy, 24
Piggly Wiggly, 125
Pioneer Hall, 76
Pious Fund of the Californias, 37
Polk, Willis, 90
Pope, George, 100
Portolá, Gaspar de, 17
Prohibition, 51, 68, 108, 121
Province of the Pacific, 79

R

Radin, Mark, 163
Ralston, Andrew Jackson, 26, 27
Ralston, William C., 36, 39, 60
Rancho de las Pulgas, 6, 17
Randolphs of Redwood, 53
Ransom, Leander, 24
Rathbone, Alejandra Atherton, 62
Rathbone, Lawrence, 63
Ravenswood, 18, 29, 44, 79
Raychem Corporation, 5
Red Cross, 13
Rincon Hill, 21, 27, 34, 36, 52
Ringwood, 9, 37
Riordan, Patrick William, 29, 62, 122
Roach, Frank, 76
Rolph, James Jr., 93
Roth, Berenice, 115
Roth, Lurline, 115
Ryan, Dominic "Dom," 149
Ryan, J. William, 149

S

Sacred Heart Schools, 78
St. Bridget's Catholic Church, 42
St. Denis Catholic Church, 164
St. Denis Church, 19, 43, 62
St. Joseph's School, 88
St. Patrick's Seminary, 12, 18, 29, 63, 64,
    79, 95
Saloons, 12, 13, 94, 95, 51, 108
Sand Hill Road, 6, 147, 171
San Francisco & San Jose Railroad, 22
San Francisco Forty-Niners, 177
San Francisco Stock Exchange, 41
San Francisquito Creek, 6, 16, 17, 19
San Mateo County Great Register, 81
San Mateo County Historical
    Association, 25
San Mateo County Memorial Park, 135
Sawyer, Houghton, 90
Schumann-Heink, Ernestine, 102, 103
Selby, Elena Atherton, 62
Selby, Henrietta Reese, 27
Selby, Jennie, 26, 27
Selby, Percy, 26, 27, 67
Selby, Thomas H., 24, 26, 27, 54
Sequoia High School, 77, 152
Seward, William, 41
Shannon, Larry, 168
Sharon, Frederick W., 82, 83, 163, 164
Sharon Heights, 82, 99, 163, 164
Sharon Heights Country Club, 163
Sharon, Louise Tevis Breckinridge, 82
Sharon, William, 82
Sherwood Hall, 10, 11, 14, 59, 63, 77,
    138, 165
Sherwood Hall Gate Lodge, 165
Sherwood Hall Nursery, 59
Shortridge, Samuel M., 85, 136
Siberia, 106, 107
Siberian Christmas Cheer Fund, 107

Signal Oil Company, 153
Silber, Bernard, 140
Silicon Valley, 171, 180
Sims, Lisa, 175
Snowden, Margaret, 158, 169
Society of Sulpice, 79
Softky, Marion, 169
Southern Pacific Railroad, 9, 10, 59,
    72, 89, 146
South Park, 30, 31
Spanish Influenza, 13, 105
SRI International (See Stanford
    Research Institute)
Stamps, Shannon, 152
Stanford Convalescent Home, 114
Stanford Dairy, 45
Stanford Free Kindergarten, 57
Stanford, Jane, 12, 25, 46, 54, 56, 57, 58,
    69, 71, 73, 113
Stanford, Leland, 9, 11, 12, 23, 46, 47, 54,
    55, 56, 67, 69, 70, 72, 73
Stanford, Leland Jr., 56, 69, 71
Stanford Memorial Arch, 69
Stanford Museum & Art Gallery, 127
Stanford Research Institute (SRI
    International), 5, 15, 144, 145, 167
Stanford Stockfarm, 71
Stanford University, 5, 10, 11, 12, 51, 56,
    62, 63, 69, 70, 72, 73, 75, 77, 94, 95,
    101, 103, 138, 145, 161, 165, 167,
    171, 178
Stern, Abraham, 90
Stern, Elise (Mrs. Walter A. Hass), 91
Stern, Jacob, 90
Stern, Louis, 90
Stern, Lucie, 90
Stern, Rosalie, 91, 104
Stern, Sigmund, 90, 91
Stillman, John M., 101
Stowe, William, 67
Suburban Park, 180
Sunset Limited, 146
Sunset Magazine, 135, 146, 147, 153
Sunset Seed & Plant Company, 59

T

Taylor, Bayard, 41
Telser, Tashana, 152
Thurlow Lodge (See also *Sherwood Hall*),
    35, 59
Time Warner, 147
Trans-Siberian Railroad, 107
Twohig, Eleanor, 119

U

Ulrich, Rudolf, 63
Unadilla, 32
U. S. Geological Survey (USGS), 5,
    161, 162
Universal Studios, 138
University Heights, 45

V

Vallombrosa, 67, 141
Vallombrosa Center, 141
Valparaiso Park, 12, 21, 52
Vaqueros, 92
Venceramos, 167
Veterans Administration Hospital, 14,
    108, 109
Victoria Loftus British Blondes
    Troupe Burlesquers, 131
Victoria Manor, 110, 111, 112, 148
Victor Talking Machine Company, 110
Violets, 11, 63
Vladivostok, 106, 107

W

Wall Meat Market, 125
Walter, Clarence, 118
Warner Bros. Studios, 138
Warren, William H., 97
Washington Mill Company, 32
Watkins, James T., 30, 31, 42
Wells, Fargo & Co., 70
Westphal, E.W., 118
Wheaton, David, 169
White, Billy Ray, 169, 181
Wilbur, Ray Lyman, 8, 148
Wildman, Helen, 61
William Warren School, 97, 148
Williams, Buzz, 177
Wilson, Albert, 136
Woods, Isaiah C., 7, 18, 29, 79
Woodside-Atherton Auxiliary, 126
Woodside Dairy, 18, 29
Works Progress Administration
    (W.P.A.), 135
Wo Sing Laundry, 75

Y

Yosemite National Park, 155